What You Can Learn

from the Breakthrough Research

to Make Your Marriage Last

SIMON & SCHUSTER

New York   London   Toronto   Sydney   Tokyo   Singapore

WHY MARRIAGES SUCCEED OR FAIL

JOHN GOTTMAN, Ph.D.
with Nan Silver

SIMON & SCHUSTER
Rockefeller Center
1230 Avenue of the Americas
New York, New York 10020

Library of Congress Cataloging-in-Publication Data

Gottman, John.
  Why marriages succeed or fail: what you can
learn from the breakthrough research to make your
marriage last / John Gottman with Nan Silver.
    p.   cm.
  1. Marriage—United States.   2. Communica-
tion in marriage—United States.   I. Silver,
Nan.   II. Title.
HQ536.G68   1994
306.81'0973—dc20   93-35891   CIP
ISBN: 0-671-86748-2

Dedicated to
All the love I know with
my wife Julie and my daughter Moriah

Two are better than one;
Because they have a good reward for their labor.
For if they fall, the one will lift up his fellow,
But woe to him that is alone when he falls,
for he has not another to help him up.
And if two lie together then they have warmth,
but how can one be warm alone?
And if one prevail against him,
two shall withstand him.

—*from* ECCLESIASTES, 1:9:12

CONTENTS

PREFACE

My personal life has not been a trail of great wisdom in understanding relationships. Indeed, I have probably experienced most of the pitfalls of ailing relationships. I finally got lucky when I met my wife, Julie Schwartz, and now have been able to experience how a marriage can flourish.

This book is not about me, nor is it just another opinion about how to have a good marriage. My expertise is in the scientific observation of couples. Over the course of more than twenty years of research with hundreds of couples, I have found that many of my personal ideas about what holds a couple together—and much of the conventional wisdom among professionals—has been wrong. But the power of doing research is that you can go far beyond your limited intuitions or the hunches of a lone therapist. With impartial observations and statistics you can hear nature tell you what is true. The couples who have participated in my studies, who share their stories in these pages, have revealed the hidden natural laws of relationships.

These couples have shared their pain, but they have also shared their joy, showing me the splendid possibilities of a relationship—the sense in which, as Ecclesiastes has it, "Two are better than one." It is as though each of us were singing a solo in some grand, mysterious choir, and our voices rose to the heavens the moment we found a partner to blend with in two-part harmony.

11

ONE

WHAT MAKES MARRIAGE WORK?

Have you and your spouse ever planned a big romantic getaway only to find that once alone together, you fall into the same argument you've had twenty times before? Maybe it's about plans for the future—whether to buy a bigger house, when or if to have a child, how to save for retirement. Or perhaps it's a past wound—the way he acted on the honeymoon, or her fling with a co-worker that ended years ago. Or it could be a never-ending debate over housework, disciplining the children, when to have sex, or how to spend vacations.

I know a woman who traveled with her husband all the way to New Zealand, only to have a nasty spat the night of their arrival. He wanted to go deep-sea diving the next day; she wanted to sun on the beach.

"Your ideas are always so reckless," she fumed. "Why can't you just act like the middle-aged man you are?"

He retaliated, "You stifle my sense of adventure," adding a note of quiet contempt: "You bore me to tears."

Soon she *was* in tears, as their cross-fire continued for about an hour, until they finally called a truce. Stinging from one another's insults, they sat there realizing a worse pain: they could travel to the end of the earth together and still be stuck in a war that started fifteen years ago, fighting the same battles over and over again.

Sound familiar? Or are you and your spouse more likely to avoid such skirmishes at all costs? Perhaps you're more like another couple I'm familiar with, who will float through such a vacation together, giving in to one another's wishes, carefully sidestepping any potential disagreement, burying past disappointments, stifling any complaints, ignoring any suggestion of conflict. If you and your spouse are this way, the odds are neither of you would say what's really on your minds; that way there's no friction and nobody gets hurt. These are peaceful matches—except for this occasional, unpredictable twinge of restlessness. It might surface, say, when he tosses his jacket over his shoulder in a certain way, or when she brushes a wisp of hair from her eyes with the back of her hand. It's these small, familiar gestures that can make you remember: *There used to be more passion here.* You wonder what happened to all the laughter and affection. When did life together become so flat and colorless?

Or, maybe, at least sometimes, your marriage is like that of another couple I know. They go out for a Sunday afternoon in town together. She wants to do some browsing in shops; he starts to get visibly impatient. She begins to sulk, thinking, "He doesn't really want to spend time with me. He's so uncaring." Meanwhile, he broods, "She's spending too much money—she's so selfish. Why can't we just enjoy going for a walk?" And for the rest of the afternoon the two are caught in separate ruminations about each other's faults.

Or, perhaps you and your mate are like still another couple, no longer even spending such time together. Come Sunday, she's caught up in a whirl of chores, helping the kids with school projects, trying to get the laundry done and the house in order; he's out playing softball, working on the car, or watching football on TV, or puttering somewhere. If your relationship has lots of times like this, the two of you may be living in parallel universes under the same roof.

And yet this is the person you loved so deeply when you got married, the person you sincerely meant to stick with through the joys and hardships of life. But despite your best wishes, there are moments when it seems impossible. It's as though some powerful, subterranean current takes hold of you both and leads you down a path of negative thinking, destructive feelings, painful action and reaction, drifting toward isolation and loneliness.

What is this mysterious current? Today, as we witness the dissolution of so many marriages, it becomes more crucial than ever to find an answer. And finding that answer has been the mission of my research these past two decades. Through intense, detailed observations of hundreds of couples like these, I have charted the invisible emotional currents between husbands and wives, underground streams of feeling that can burst to the surface either as a spring of harmony or a well of discontent.

In pursuit of the truth about what tears a marriage apart or binds it together, I have found that much of the conventional wisdom— even among many marital therapists—is misguided or dead wrong. For example, some marital patterns that even professionals often take as a sign of a problem—such as having intense fights, or avoiding conflict altogether—I have found can signify highly successful adjustments that will keep a couple together. And fighting—when it airs grievances and complaints—can be one of the healthiest things a couple can do for their relationship (indeed, how you fight is one of the most telling ways to diagnose the health of your marriage). You will see more clearly why such conventional assumptions are dead wrong as you read my explanation of the often elusive emotional dynamics of marriage, dynamics I have mapped in a simple model that can serve as a template for seeing your own marriage with new eyes.

The good news is that if you become familiar with these maps of what shapes the emotional currents in marriage for better or worse, the seemingly elusive forces that are at work in your own relationship need not be so mysterious to you, nor are you at their mercy anymore. In this book I will show you how to detect these forces in your own relationship so that you can see the hidden emotional profile of your marriage as though through an X ray. By making these hidden forces visible, you can start to control the direction of your marital journey— calling a final truce on destructive arguments, corrosive ways of thinking about each other, and the downward spiral of reactions that can destroy a marriage. Instead, you can open the door to a more vital, fulfilling relationship.

DEMYSTIFYING THE MARRIAGE CRISIS

If you are worried about the future of your marriage you have plenty of company. There's no denying that this is a frightening time for American couples. More than half of all first marriages end in divorce. Second marriages do worse, failing at a rate of about 60 percent. Although many social scientists believed that divorce rates had leveled off in the 1980s, new data suggest the opposite: the divorce rate is actually getting worse as time goes on. A 1989 study of U.S. Census records by researchers at the University of Wisconsin found that, based on 1985 data, divorce among *recent* first marriages stood at a shocking *67 percent*. In other words, two out of every three new couples are headed for divorce—unless something changes. That "something" is what this book is about—how to change your marriage to save it.

There's no question that the statistics are distressing, especially if you fear that your own marriage may be in danger. What makes the numbers even more disturbing is that no one seems to understand *why* our marriages have become so fragile. It is as if some hidden, evil force is loose in America that is making marriages fall apart. But the reason marriage and its troubles seem so mysterious is really quite simple: until recently, almost no scientific studies of this complex relationship had been done. The vast majority of books of advice to couples have been based, at best, on the insights marital therapists have gained from the couples they happened to see, and, at worst, on mere anecdote and theoretical musings.

And most of the research on marriage has suffered, in my opinion, from a number of flaws ranging from asking the wrong questions to conclusions that are simply not valid. The solution, of course, is to conduct solid experiments that examine stable and troubled marriages, systematically tracing the emotional currents that lead one couple to drift apart and another to flow through life together. For the past two decades my research teams have been doing just that. The result has been a number of surprising, scientifically sound findings that go a long way to filling in the knowledge gap. I have written this book to share our latest results with you and to offer my best understanding of just how you can strengthen your marriage, no matter how rocky it may seem.

Of course, not all couples ought to stay married. But I do think it's disturbing that the majority of people marrying today will be unsuccessful at nurturing and holding onto their most precious relationship—all the more disturbing because, I believe, an accurate diagnosis of the fault lines in a marriage can help any couple build a stronger union.

On your wedding day you had hopes for a happy, blissful union, and I believe that despite the rising divorce rate you can still fulfill that dream—even if your marriage has started to show signs of trouble. Although our research is far from complete, our current findings offer the most accurate picture available of why some marriages succeed and others fail—and what you can do to improve your own chances of ending up on the positive side of the odds.

BOB AND WENDY: THE PIONEERS

Early in my career as a psychologist, a young couple came to me for help with their ailing marriage. Bob and Wendy, as I'll call them, were a passionate, loving pair who had been attracted to each other's opposite nature. Wendy was energetic, spontaneous, and had a flair for design. Bob was more conservative, intellectual, with a penchant for order. He loved her vivaciousness and found her exciting—"a bit of a gypsy." She was drawn to his reason, his dependability, his even temper.

But once they were married with a child, the stresses of family life began to bear down. Wendy worked full time in a fast-paced media job. Bob was struggling to get through graduate school while caring for the baby and the house. By the time I met them, rather than marveling in the charms that had drawn them together, they had begun to disdain one another's habits.

"I don't know how you can be so sloppy," Bob fumed. "You don't even appreciate all the work I do to maintain your house."

"*My* house?" Wendy countered. "We both live here, but because I'm a woman, you automatically assume that housework is *my* responsibility."

"That's not true," was his comeback. "It's just that *you've* done all the decorating. I don't give a damn about all this furniture and all this . . . stuff! I'm just doing my best to keep up."

"So it's *my* fault that you don't value living in a beautiful environment? You know what your problem is? You're always afraid of anything the least bit adventurous or new!"

And so it went day after day. Despite their best intentions, conversations seemed to deteriorate into an endless loop of criticism over housework, child care, and personal habits. And once they took their positions, they felt trapped, as if there was no way to break out of their defensiveness and anger. One day, on a hunch, I suggested that we videotape their discussions so I could take a closer look at the dynamics of their interaction.

We made three tapes in all. For the first one, I proposed that they play a game called "The NASA Moon Shot Problem," in which two people rank in order a set of items needed for survival on a trip to the moon. Here, the couple shined. They had a lively, productive discussion, filled with lots of laughs. They got superb scores for cooperation and problem solving. But perhaps more important, their affection for one another was palpable. Clearly, this was the pair who had met years ago and fallen in love.

With the second tape, however, the harmony faded. I asked them to discuss a major problem in their marriage, and before long, they were back to bickering, pouting, whining, feeling angry and bitter. The third session, which they recorded on an audiotape at home, was even worse. They rehashed the same issues over and over again. Each time they got anywhere near a solution, one of them inevitably would sabotage the process. When the tape finally ended, Bob and Wendy were exhausted and full of despair.

I watched and listened to these tapes over and over again. Then I listened to them with Bob and Wendy. I asked them to tell me what they were thinking and feeling at certain critical or puzzling moments in the conversation. What I detected hidden beneath their seemingly trivial skirmishes was a rich and painful history of unresolved issues concerning his need for autonomy and her need to feel valued by him. I learned that Bob and Wendy, like most couples I've worked with over the years, really wanted just two things from their marriage— love and respect. But, also like so many distressed couples, their communication had become distorted. With increasing frequency, they would find themselves cornered into interactions where all each one could hear was the other one's criticism and contempt. The recurring episodes scared both of them. Although neither one wanted to divorce, each feared that's where they were headed.

Still, Bob and Wendy were committed to saving their marriage and they had gained insights about their interactions from our work together. Determined to find better ways to express their needs to one another, they worked hard in therapy. When I last saw them some twenty years ago, they seemed to be on track toward a more stable relationship. And, thanks in part to their willingness to help me with this videotaped experiment, I was on a new track as well. I was determined to find out why some marriages fall apart while other marriages thrive. I felt that a better understanding of the destructive interactions that lead to divorce might help save couples who feel trapped in a downward spiral of hostility and bitterness.

PREDICTING DIVORCE

This was uncharted territory in the early 1970s, a time when divorce rates were already soaring. There was a plethora of psychological theories about how to fix broken marriages. The problem was these theories were based mostly on psychologists' intuition and experience with their own clients. That's not to say their ideas were bad. But preventing divorce can be compared to preventing heart disease. You wouldn't rely solely on the knowledge of a doctor who had treated a dozen heart attacks; you'd turn to a body of scientific work based on carefully designed experiments with hundreds of people—some with heart disease and others without. The same could be said for treating the heartbreak of a marriage in distress. But this sound, systematic research had not been conducted among divorced and stable couples, to tease out the differences between them. Trained as a mathematician and a research psychologist, I decided to take such an approach. Using scientific methods, I would observe the conversations of husbands and wives, distilling out of the mists and confusions of anger, frustration, and isolation the differences that lead some couples to stay married and others to divorce.

Two decades later, this strategy has reaped an enormous reward. For the first time we can name with precision the subtle early warning signs of a troubled marriage, and tell you how to put these insights to good use, setting your own marriage on the right track and keeping it there for years to come.

X RAY OF A MARRIAGE

My laboratory conducts what amounts to the most intensive studies of couples interacting ever attempted, something akin to an X ray or CAT scan of a living relationship. My research teams have compared, microsecond to microsecond, how couples talk to one another. We've examined their facial expressions, monitored how much they fidget, and how they gesture. We've asked what happens to partners' heart rates when they try to work out their conflicts together. Do unstable couples express more sarcasm or contempt in these situations than stable couples? Do they breathe harder? Do they find it more difficult to listen? How well do they understand one another's emotions? And what about discrepancies in the way couples describe the history of their relationships? Does it make any difference if he recalls she wore yellow the first time he saw her? Does it matter whether they laugh when they reminisce about hard times?

What we have found is that all of this matters. What's more, gathering such information has allowed us to identify the specific processes that lead to the dissolution of a marriage, and those that weld it more firmly together. To use the heart disease analogy again, preventing heart attacks requires an ability to predict the events leading up to the crisis: plaque formation on arteries, high blood pressure, chest pain, and so on. Divorce prevention requires this same foresight. That's why I have geared my research to identifying which responses, thoughts, and physiological reactions place couples on a path toward divorce. In doing so, we have been able to predict with startling accuracy which couples will stay together and which couples will split. In one study, for example, we were able to foretell with an astonishing *94 percent* accuracy which couples were headed for divorce three years later, based solely on couples' views of their marital history and their current perceptions. That remains the highest prediction rate ever achieved by a scientific study on marriage!

I don't mean to imply that our findings are foolproof, nor that every couple who experiences certain problems is inevitably headed for divorce. The predictions of marital outcome in my research were arrived at after about twenty hours of direct laboratory observation and contact with each couple, and even then the predictions were not perfect. Many couples who at one point in marriage have difficulties are able to find their way to a stable, satisfying marriage.

But being aware that specific patterns and interactions in your marriage are part of a process that leads to divorce—and knowing how to reverse those patterns—may indeed help you back away from that slippery slope. It's in this spirit of prevention that I offer you advice about improving your marriage. I do so with some hesitation because I know that my research is not yet finished; the dynamics of marriage are complex and I feel we have much to explore. Still, we have learned a tremendous amount from comparing how couples treat each other in thriving and failing relationships. I hope that by sharing our insights with you, we can help you improve your marriage today, and help it last through many tomorrows.

OLD MYTHS DIE HARD

Over the years, plenty of theories have attempted to explain the underlying cause of the surge in divorce. Read through popular and psychological literature and you'll find your pick of culprits. Some social scientists point to our society's shift from a family farm economy to factories, which undercut the importance of family, as the core of the problem. Others have blamed changes in law that make divorce easier, or women's emerging financial independence, which enables wives to leave bad marriages more easily. Some experts point to our society's increasing levels of violence; the psychological abuses of contempt and hostility that often precede divorce may be considered a low-level form of violence.

Looked at together, these explanations point to a weakening of the social threads that keep marriages intact. But they don't explain why some marriages last despite these pressures while others disintegrate. These speculations don't help you very much if you are trying to navigate your way through marital difficulty. If you are currently married or planning to marry, what you most want to know is how to avoid falling on the sad side of the statistics.

Because there hasn't been much solid research on why specific marriages fall apart, we're tempted to believe comfortable old notions that, on the surface, seem quite plausible. Take the money myth, for example. Some figures show that if you have financial difficulties you are twice as susceptible to divorce. But many couples with low incomes stay together. You can earn $15,000 a year and have a marriage as solid or shaky as couples making $150,000. In his book, *Children of the Great Depression*, G. H. Elder, Jr., gives an interesting account of how money problems affected families in the 1930s. Those who were strong couples before the stock market crashed seemed to become even stronger afterward, as wives and children chipped in to help support the family. On the other hand, families that were already troubled were more likely to be torn apart by economic strife. Husbands in troubled marriages moved further and further away from their families at the dinner table as financial problems worsened—a concrete expression of the widening distance between husband and wife. In essence, such studies show that your marriage's existing strengths or weaknesses simply get amplified by external crises like unemployment or money problems.

Similar conclusions can be drawn about sexual disagreements, which are also widely held to be marriage busters. Long ago, some psychologists believed the more often you and your partner had intercourse, the happier you'd be. We know now this isn't true; what really matters is that you agree on what's acceptable. Remember the scene from the movie *Annie Hall*? When Annie's therapist asks her how often she and Alvie have sex, she replies, "Constantly. Three times a week." Alvie's therapist asks him the same question and he answers, "Never. Three times a week." The issue isn't how frequently you make love—nor even that you agree that sex 1.43 times a week is optimum. The issue is how well you handle the inevitable differences that arise whenever two people form a partnership.

A closely related myth holds that compatibility—both in and out of bed—is the bottom line when it comes to making your marriage work. Say you love to spend your leisure time surrounded by family and friends, but your mate would rather stay home alone with you. Or you think credit cards are a gift from God while your partner believes in paying as you go. Maybe you feel day-care centers are fine even though your spouse is convinced that babies belong at home with their mothers. The marriage counselor's prediction: trouble ahead.

At first glance, it seems to make sense that compatibility would be a necessary foundation for a successful marriage. Take the research conducted by David H. Olson, professor of family social science at the University of Minnesota. He has developed a premarital test called PREPARE that detects differences between prospective husbands and wives. Administered by clergy during premarital counseling, this 125-item questionnaire covers eleven areas of the couple's life including personality issues, finances, sexual matters, children, and religious orientation. The goal is to predict areas of conflict in a marriage, supposedly to avoid disharmony and eventual divorce. Olson's questionnaire does a fairly good job of identifying potential hot spots and predicting marital satisfaction. Checking in on couples three years after they were married, Olson reported that those who were currently satisfied had indeed scored higher on the PREPARE test before their wedding than those who were dissatisfied or divorced.

What his evaluation could *not* predict, however, was which among the many *dissatisfied* couples in his study were destined to stay married and which were headed for a fall. This is the crucial question. After all, many marriages that are basically stable go through occasional periods of dissatisfaction. You must know people who find their marriages less than ideal yet stay together for a lifetime, or couples who are quite dissimilar but find their marriages very satisfying. And you probably know others who remain in marriages that are full of conflict because they find the rewards worth the battle.

Olson assumed similarity in opinions safeguards against divorce. That does not seem to be true. In my research, where I actually observed couples hashing out disagreements and then tracked them down years later to check on how stable their marriages were, I found that couples who initially had complaints about each other's attitudes were among the most stable marriages as the years went on. My research shows that much more important than having compatible views is *how* couples work out their differences. In fact, occasional discontent, especially during a marriage's early years, seems be good for the union in the long run.

Clearly, marital bliss and perfect compatibility are not the only glue that holds couples together—and may not even be the most important glue. The challenge for my research teams has been to identify the truly crucial ingredients to a sound marriage. That's quite a tall order. It required us to follow marriages over a very long period of time. There is simply no shortcut to staying in touch with the same couples for many years if you want to find out which will go on to live happy, fulfilled lives together and which will end up separating.

IN THE MARRIAGE LAB

It's 6:30 on a Thursday night when Phil and Diane Thompson (not their real names) arrive at our facilities on the University of Washington campus in Seattle. After walking down a spare corridor in the office building that houses our lab, they seem surprised to see what lies before them: a comfortably furnished studio apartment, complete with a hide-a-bed, kitchen facilities, and a view of the canal that connects Portage Bay to Lake Washington. Once inside, the only clues that the Thompsons haven't escaped to some cozy Northwest getaway are the three remote-control video cameras perched in corners of the ceiling. It's here that we observe couples who want to get at the heart of what makes their marriage tick.

After a brief get-acquainted session with two research assistants, the Thompsons complete a form that asks them to describe how much they disagree about topics that often trouble couples—issues like money, in-laws, sex, and religion. By now the couple is used to such probing questions; as volunteer study participants, they've already responded to several questionnaires and interviews regarding the state of their marriage. If they continue their involvement in our research, they'll receive phone calls and questionnaires from time to time, asking them about the status of their relationship. This is how we track the progress of couples over the years.

Once they fill out the form, the Thompsons are taken to an adjacent room to be seated in opposing chairs surrounded by an array of electronic equipment specially designed to gather physical and psychological information about couples as they interact. A shifting platform beneath each chair measures how much each partner wiggles during the session. Two more video cameras are suspended above, filming every visible movement from the waist up.

"This feels like an electric chair," Phil jokes, as a research assistant wraps a strap across his chest to measure how deeply he's breathing.

"Or a lie detector," Diane muses. Actually, she's got it right. Various electronic gadgets will measure the nervous system's response to all sorts of psychological stimuli in much the same way that a polygraph test would. Electrodes are placed on the pair's chests to track heart rates. Devices are taped to their fingers, monitoring their pulse and how much they sweat in response to stress. Sensors are clipped to their ear lobes to tell how fast blood flows from their hearts to their extremities. Finally, microphones are hung from their clothes to capture every sound they utter.

When all the equipment is arranged, a research assistant reviews the questionnaire with Phil and Diane, helping them to decide which "area of disagreement" they will discuss for fifteen minutes. (In some of our studies, the couple begins by simply discussing the events of their day, after having been apart for at least eight hours.) According to Phil and Diane's answers, sex is a problem in their relationship; conflicts arise because Phil wants to make love more frequently than Diane does. Both agree it's a topic ripe for discussion.

This decided, the staff members disappear into an adjoining room stacked with computer equipment and video monitors. As instructed, the couple sits quietly for five minutes while the researchers gather baseline data. Then a blinking light on a nearby display panel appears—the couple's cue to begin talking.

They start by discussing their respective families. Neither were terrific models of affection, they agree. Then the subject switches to their courtship. They reminisce about the thrill of those first few months, and how the magic faded. Soon, Diane is complaining about Phil's work, which seems to consume him. She says if he would express more affection outside the bedroom, maybe she'd find the prospect of sex more appealing. Phil falls silent for a while and then brings up their child. "Things might be better if you didn't let Jason stay up until eleven o'clock every night." Diane concedes that Jason is an obstacle. Then she suggests that they get some books on love-making. Phil offers a weak smile. "We've been over all this before," he sighs.

When fifteen minutes have passed, the light on the panel fades and a research assistant reappears. She sets up a screen to block the couple's view of one another. She directs their attention to a video monitor where they can see a split-screen image of the conversation that's just transpired. Using a dial that turns 180 degrees from "positive" to "neutral" to "negative," Phil and Diane watch the tape twice. The first time, they rate their own feelings at the time the conversation unfolded—how positive or negative they felt moment to moment. The second time, they use the dial to guess how their partner was feeling minute by minute. This exercise evaluates how accurately the couple can "read" one another's emotions.

Later, the same tape will be viewed by psychologists specially trained to analyze the emotional content of people's words, facial expressions, and gestures. Using a dial with settings that range from "disgust," "contempt," and "belligerence" to "validation," "affection," and "joy," these researchers will code every moment of the conversation, assigning a label to each nuance. If a researcher sees Diane's lips tighten when Phil mentions her permissiveness with Jason, the record will register her anger and just how long it lasted. If Phil sighs deeply as she tells him she wishes he would work less, the record will show his sadness. And if either one shuts down, unable or unwilling to respond to what the other is saying, there will be a record of withdrawal as well.

These codes, when correlated with data from the couple's physiological responses, as well as their answers to various questionnaires and interviews, produce a gold mine of information about a couple's interaction. Combined with a multitude of data we've collected from hundreds of other couples in the past two decades, Phil and Diane's simple conversation lends tremendous insight to our understanding of the hidden emotional dynamics of marriage. It is from this mountain of data that I have distilled a scientific model of the often invisible forces that hold a marriage together or tear it apart—a model I want to share with you, so you can get a reading of these forces in your own marriage.

THE STUDIES

I first refined the methods used to measure Phil and Diane's interaction at Indiana University in 1980, when I teamed up with Robert W. Levenson, a scientist with considerable expertise in measuring physiological responses in social situations. Studying the interactions of thirty married couples, Levenson and I proved for the first time that marital satisfaction is linked to spouses' physiological responses to one another. But these experiments were significant in another regard as well. They showed us that it was indeed possible to get couples to act naturally toward one another despite the intrusion of video cameras, electrodes, and microphones. Amazing as it sounds, once these couples were in our lab and put at ease by our assistants, the wires, transducers, and cameras seemed to recede into the background, and their interactions showed the full range of authentic emotions displayed by married couples in "real-life" conversations.

Confident that our methods worked and our findings were valid, we then began a long-term study to see what happens to marriages over time. Was it possible to pinpoint certain behaviors or processes that lead to divorce? What are these factors and, once they are identified, can we use them to predict which couples will stay married and which couples will split? Seventy-nine couples of all different ages came to our observation lab in 1983 to help us find these answers. Checking back with them in 1987, we found links between the information we collected in 1983 and the couples' marital status four years later. Further analysis allowed us to understand in great detail the processes that lead to the dissolution of marriage. These findings were repeated in a similar study I conducted at the University of Illinois with fifty-six couples beginning in 1986. These two studies continue to yield results as we contact both the Indiana and Illinois couples periodically for updates on the state of their relationships.

In the meantime, two new studies are under way. In one, we are following 130 newlywed couples for at least five years to find out how the arrival of children affects their relationships. A second new study, conducted with Robert Levenson at the University of California at Berkeley and Laura Carstensen at Stanford University, involves 160 marriages among couples now in their forties and sixties, who have never divorced. These folks have been married for an average of twenty and forty years, respectively. Our goal is to learn more about how people manage successful, long-term relationships. For example, we're taking a close look at their capacity to break away from defensive behavior in the middle of an argument and get their conversations back on a more productive track.

What does all this have to do with your marriage? This growing body of research has taught me a great deal that may help you improve your marriage. To benefit from this insight, you needn't hook yourself up to wires or videotape your fights the way we do with couples in our lab. Rather, this book will share with you the essence of what I've learned over the years, and show you practical ways you can put our findings to work in your own relationship.

CONFLICT: A KEY TO HAPPINESS?

If there is one lesson I have learned from my years of research it is that *a lasting marriage results from a couple's ability to resolve the conflicts that are inevitable in any relationship*. Many couples tend to equate a low level of conflict with happiness and believe the claim "we never fight" is a sign of marital health. But I believe we grow in our relationships by reconciling our differences. That's how we become more loving people and truly experience the fruits of marriage.

But there's much more to know than how to fight well. Not all stable couples resolve conflicts in the same way. Nor do all couples mean the same thing by "resolving" the conflict. In fact, I have found that there are three different styles of problem solving into which healthy marriages tend to settle. In a *validating marriage* couples compromise often and calmly work out their problems to mutual satisfaction as they arise. In a *conflict-avoiding marriage* couples agree to disagree, rarely confronting their differences head-on. And finally, in a *volatile marriage* conflicts erupt often, resulting in passionate disputes.

Previously, many psychologists might have considered conflict-avoiding and volatile marriages to be pathological. But our current research suggests that all three styles are equally stable and bode equally well for the marriage's future. In chapter 2, I will go into detail about these three styles and help you decide which is closest to the marriage you currently have or would *like* to have.

Of course, following one of these three styles won't guarantee a happy marriage. These adaptations work only to the degree that they allow you to achieve the right balance between positive and negative interactions with your spouse. Amazingly, we have found that it all comes down to a simple mathematical formula: no matter what style your marriage follows, you must have at least five times as many positive as negative moments together if your marriage is to be stable.

If you and your spouse do not arrive at a stable equilibrium, when this balance, or "marital ecology," becomes upset, you and your mate will find yourselves frustrated, sniping or lost in a dead end, quarreling more and more. These are the signs of the failure to find a stable marital style you both find comfortable.

In chapters 3 and 4, I will map out for you the downward spiral that begins in couples who are unable to find the equilibrium of a stable type of marriage. And in chapter 5 I will show how strong differences between men and women in how they handle emotions can feed this process. Negativity builds, with increasingly damaging results. It begins as laughter and validation disappear, and criticism and pain well up. Your attempts to soothe one another's hurt feelings and get communication back on track seem useless. Partners become lost in hostile and negative thoughts and feelings, as their bodies react to the stress, making it harder to think rationally, to respond calmly. Soon, the destructive interactions I call "The Four Horsemen of the Apocalypse" take over. They are criticism, contempt, defensiveness, and withdrawal. At this point, unless a couple makes changes, they are likely to find themselves sliding helplessly toward the end of their marriage. In chapter 6, I'll help you review the results of your analysis of your own marriage, to see the ways in which these destructive forces have begun to eat away at your marriage.

Is the solution simply to be nice the next time your spouse insults your sister, readjusts the thermostat, shrinks your favorite shirt, or engages in some other crazy-making behavior? Hardly. But there are specific steps you *can* take to resolve conflicts constructively and strengthen the positive side of your marriage. And if you follow them regularly, they should inoculate your relationship against the forces that can lead to divorce.

These steps—outlined in detail in the second half of this book—include communication techniques that proved to stabilize marriages in therapy studies I conducted among couples at Indiana University in the late 1970s. Several researchers, including Howard Markman, a psychologist at the University of Denver and a former student, and Neil Jacobson at the University of Washington, have corroborated my early findings: learning these strategies counters the destructive tactics that can tear a marriage apart. Couples who master these crucial techniques—particularly how to settle disagreements without escalating conflict—are strengthening their marriages.

My method of diagnosing the fault lines in a marriage, and the advice that follows, spring from scientific data collected from hundreds of couples, and they represent the most complete information available anywhere about the way men and women interact in marriages that succeed and in marriages that fail.

If you choose to follow the steps outlined in this book, keep in mind that they are not band-aid solutions. They will require vigilance and commitment, and they may involve changing the way you perceive yourself, your partner, and your relationship. They may also require you to change how you habitually listen and react to your spouse. Most of all, you'll need to work at making these new, more productive habits so familiar that they will be automatic responses when you need them the most: at the difficult, tense moments between you and your spouse. To do this, you'll need a thorough understanding of where your relationship stands today. That's why the book also includes several tests to help you assess and diagnose what kind of marriage you prefer, as well as the character of your present bond. These tests are not meant to predict whether you're headed for divorce, but they can help you identify the trouble spots in a way that will clarify the antidotes you need to try. In the second half of the book, each of the difficulties you've diagnosed in your marriage will be matched with a specific remedy, something you can change to strengthen your marriage.

Marriage is an extremely complex relationship and there is no single test that can predict its survival or dissolution with 100 percent accuracy. You and your partner are the only ones who know the sacrifices and rewards of your marriage, and you are the only ones who can decide its future. I hope this book can help you make thoughtful choices, and identify and change the emotional currents that if left unchecked, can undermine a marriage.

TWO

MARRIAGE STYLES:
THE GOOD, THE BAD,
AND THE VOLATILE

Late at night, countless TV sets around the nation still tune in to watch Ralph and Alice go at it on reruns of *The Honeymooners*. His take-no-prisoners attacks and her smart-alecky comebacks have reduced generations of Americans to belly laughs. There's something about the marital explosions that detonate in their sparse Brooklyn living room that so many of us find endearing and entertaining.

You probably know of at least one couple like the Cramdens. These high-decibel twosomes often entertain their unfortunate neighbors with ear-shattering discussions about whether to buy solid or chunk-style tuna, or put 60- or 75-watt bulbs above the medicine cabinet. Most psychologists would probably call such frequent verbal sniping dysfunctional, even pathological. For years, marriage counselors have tried to steer couples away from this sort of bickering, convinced that it poisons a marriage.

It's certainly true that few people would aspire to a union fraught with so much tension and strife—but here's the surprise: there are couples whose fights are as deafening as the Honeymooners' yet who have long-lasting, happy marriages. If you had made that claim to me before I began my research I would have found it unlikely. But after years of tracking married couples of all sorts I have discovered that what makes a relationship work, or fall apart, is far from obvious. Some of our traditional notions of marital stability may be misguided. To see this for yourself, try your hand at predicting which of the following three newly married couples I studied remained happily married some four years later.

COUPLE NUMBER ONE

Bert and Betty Oliver, both thirty, met at a friend's wedding. For a year they sustained a long-distance romance complete with frequent plane trips and multipage phone bills. Eventually Betty moved from Cincinnati to Chicago to be with Bert and they married six months later. Bert works long, grueling hours as manager of a printing plant, a circumstance that puts some stress on their marriage. Both said they came from families where the parents weren't very communicative or intimate. Bert and Betty were determined to learn from their parents' mistake and made communication a priority in their relationship. Although they squabbled occasionally, they usually addressed their differences before the anger boiled over. Rather than shouting matches, they dealt with disagreements by having "conferences" in which each person aired his or her perspective. They tried to be understanding of each other's point of view and usually were able to arrive at a compromise. Married only two years when first interviewed, Betty expressed delight that she had been able to find that elusive creature: "a truly nice man." Bert still considered himself lucky that someone as lovely as Betty was interested in him.

COUPLE NUMBER TWO

Max Connell, forty, and Anita Gallo, twenty-five, were also married about two years when first interviewed. Max, a carpenter, met Anita on the job—he was doing repairs at a home where she was working as a nanny. In the beginning, Max was concerned that Anita would consider him too old, but she said his age was one of the things that initially attracted her. What immediately caught Max's eye was Anita's expressiveness—whatever she was feeling, she let him know. "If I try to put something off that's bothering me for maybe two days, there will be a major explosion," Anita explained. "Instead, I have to deal with it right away." Both admitted that they quarreled far more than the average couple. Their engagement was marked by so many turf wars that twice they came close to calling off the wedding. Even after marrying, they tended to interrupt each other and defend their own viewpoint rather than listen to what their partner was expressing. Eventually, however, they would reach some sort of accord. Despite their frequent tension, they seemed to take much delight in each other. They spent far more of their time together laughing, joking, and being physically affectionate than they did squabbling. Both considered passion and independence crucial factors in their lives together. They acknowledged that they had their problems, but like Bert and Betty, considered themselves happily married.

COUPLE NUMBER THREE

The Nelsons, Joe, twenty-nine, and Sheila, twenty-seven, seemed as closely paired as matching bookends. Both grew up in the suburbs of St. Louis, went to private schools, considered church-going a major focus of their lives, and were devoted to horseback riding. They said they thought alike about most everything and felt an "instant comfort" from the start. The Nelsons spent a good deal of time apart—he in his basement workshop and she in her sewing room where she devoted herself to cross-stitching. Still, they enjoyed each other's company and fought very rarely. "Not that we always agree," Sheila explained, "but we're not into conflict." When tension did arise, both considered a solo jogging session around the local country club more helpful in soothing the waters than talking things out or arguing. Asked about their major areas of tension, they gave a short list of relatively trivial concerns such as Sheila's tardiness or Joe's lack of interest in weekend chores when a Cardinals game was on TV. Sheila also mentioned as if in passing that Joe wanted to have sex far more frequently than she did, a situation that remained unresolved. In all, Joe and Sheila were proud of how well they got along. They knew that in some marriages opposites attract—"We have friends that are like that and it does work," said Sheila. "But that's not for us," Joe added.

If you guessed that couple number one, Betty and Bert Oliver, were still happily married four years later, you are right. If you guessed the same for couple number two, Anita and Max, or number three, the Nelsons, you are right again and again. If you thought only Bert and

Betty were going to make it, then you're probably a clinical psychologist or have read plenty of books and articles on what makes a marriage work. Marriages like theirs, which emphasize communication and compromise, have long been held up as the ideal. Yet, after tracking the fate of so many couples over the years, I have had to reject the notion that there is only one type of successful marriage. Rather, I believe that marriages settle into one of five different styles over time. While two of these types do lead to marital dissolution, there are three very different styles that are quite stable. Bert and Betty, Anita and Max, and Joe and Sheila are examples of these three successful marital adaptations. In other words, each represents a very specific kind of marriage that our research has linked to long term stability and happiness. The closer a marriage comes to settling into one of these three adaptations, the better its chances for permanency seem to be.

One important way we identify what type of marriage a couple has is by how they fight. Although there are other dimensions that are telling about a union, the intensity of argument seems to bring out a marriage's true colors. To classify a marriage, we look at the frequency of fights, the facial expressions and physiological responses (such as pulse rate and amount of sweating) of both partners during the confrontation, as well as what they say to each other and their tone of voice. Using these observations as our guideposts, we have named the three types of stable marriages based on their style of combat: validating, volatile, or avoidant. To find out which of these styles might work best for you, take the self-test on page 51.

BETTY AND BERT: VALIDATING

There are good reasons why Bert and Betty are close to a marriage counselor's ideal: they are virtuosos at communication. Even when discussing a hot topic, they display a lot of ease and calm. Most of all they have a keen ability to listen to and understand the other's point of view and emotions. That's why I call couples like Betty and Bert *validators*: in the midst of disagreement they still let their partner know that they consider his or her opinions and emotions valid, even if they don't agree with them. For example, here's what happened when Betty confronted Bert with a problem.

BETTY: There's one thing that's bugging me. It seems like we never do anything on the weekends. It's been so long since we've gotten together with friends, or just gone to a movie or something.

BERT: You wish we went out more often.

BETTY: Yeah. Sometimes by the end of the week I'm crawling the walls. And I just want to go out and have a good time. But then you get home Friday night and you're tired and all you want to do is watch TV and go to sleep.

BERT: Uh- huh.

BETTY: And then on Saturday and Sunday you fill up the time with chores and then you don't want to go out.

BERT: Well, you know, for me . . . I'm at the plant every day, with long hours. And when I get home I just want to be home!

BETTY: Yeah, home at last!

BERT: Right. I just want no demands, no pressures, just to hang out.

BETTY: I see.

When Betty first brought up her complaint that she wanted to go out more, there were a number of ways Bert could have responded. He could have pooh-poohed her concern, denied there was a problem, gotten angry, or immediately jumped in with his opinion. Instead, he listened to her point of view, even reflecting back to her what he heard her saying. When validating couples air their differences you tend to hear a lot of "Mmm-hmms" and "I sees." Often, the listener will also mirror the speaker's facial expressions of worry and distress. But this validation doesn't necessarily mean the partner agrees. Rather, the listener is saying, "Okay, go on. I'm interested and listening to your feelings. I may have my own point of view on this issue, but I want to hear yours." Betty offers Bert the same courtesy. Once she's said her piece, she supports him while he gives his point of view—that he's just too tired to want to go out.

This expression of mutual respect tends to limit the number of arguments couples need to have. Validator couples, we've found, tend to pick their battles carefully. Those flare-ups that do occur end up sounding more like a problem-solving discussion than a hostile call to arms.

Although not every validator argument follows a similar script, these couples do tend to display a particular pattern during their conflicts, whatever the topic. In fact, this pattern is one of the identifying characteristics of a validating couple. Usually they begin by listening as each other says their piece, as Betty and Bert did. Once they both feel they have fully aired their opinions, they move to phase two: attempting to persuade each other of the rightness of their position.

BETTY: But wouldn't it be relaxing to go out to a nice dinner, just the two of us? Or see a movie? You used to think so.

BERT: I just don't feel like it anymore. Maybe because I'm under so much pressure, it's most relaxing just to, you know . . .

BETTY: Relax.

BERT: Yeah. Don't you think so?

BETTY: (*Laughs*) No way!

Though they still don't see eye to eye, their attempts to convince each other are good-natured. There is no arm-twisting or insistence that their perspective alone is valid.

Finally, in the third phase, they negotiate a compromise both like or can at least live with.

BERT: Okay, so what do you suggest?

BETTY: Well, I think we should go out sometimes. But what happens is that I feel bad asking you 'cause you look so tired. And if I do say something you'll get angry.

BERT: Yeah. Well, you know. I'm afraid you're gonna jump on me all the time. That if I walk in the door with a big smile, you'll think I'm ready to go party and we'll be going out every night.

BETTY: So you think if you don't act really tired then I'm gonna constantly be pressuring you to go out?

BERT: Yeah, I guess I do.

BETTY: But I don't have to go out every weekend. It's just that right now we're not going out at all!

BERT: Okay. Well, how 'bout you agree that we won't go out more than, say, four times a month?

BETTY: For now.

BERT: Right.

BETTY: And then we'll definitely go out those four times.

BERT: Yeah, as long as you want to.

BETTY: You've got a deal.

As part of resolving the issue in a way that satisfied both of them, Bert and Betty got at the fundamental cause of the conflict: that Bert feared if he didn't fend off Betty by emphasizing how tired he was, they would go out far more often than he felt comfortable with. As a consequence, he acted so exhausted that they didn't go out at all. Although this sort of psychological insight is not always a part of conflict resolution in a validating couple, it is common.

In studying validating couples we have found that they tend to share other characteristics as well as the *validation/persuasion/compromise* sequence of argument. Research by Mary Anne Fitzpatrick of the University of Wisconsin on couples very similar to validators found that there is a fair amount of stereotypical sex roles in these marriages. In other words, each spouse has a separate sphere of influence. The wife is usually in charge of the home and children. The husband is usually the final decision maker. While he tends to see himself as analytical, dominant, and assertive, she views herself as nurturing, warm, and expressive. Validating couples seem to be good friends who value the "we-ness" of their marriage over their individual goals and values. It's not uncommon for them to finish each other's sentences. Among the qualities they value highly in their relationship are communication, verbal openness, being in love, displaying affection, sharing their time, activities, and interests with each other. These couples tend to consider "what's mine is yours." In their homes, they rarely have off-limit zones or a great need for privacy.

Of course, validating couples don't necessarily have marriages made in heaven. Even happy unions have their share of problems. I suspect the risk for validating couples is that they may turn their marriage into a passionless arrangement in which romance and selfhood are sacrificed for friendship and togetherness. In such a scenario they may end up forgoing personal development in favor of keeping their bond strong. I have noticed that when these couples do argue, the topic often has to do with balancing individual desires with the shared needs of the marriage. For example, one husband wanted to spend more time painting and acting, but his wife worried that his creative pursuits would squeeze out his time with her and the children. In another couple, the wife felt guilty if she spent a night out with her friends who her husband didn't like. Even though he assured her that he didn't mind, she remained unconvinced.

Still, a validating marriage appears likely to be a solid one. And that probably shouldn't be surprising. After all, when both partners feel their grievances get a sympathetic hearing, compromise is a lot easier.

MAX AND ANITA: VOLATILE

ANITA: I think that everything that we talk about, in every aspect of our relationship practically, we're always competing. Like if I say I had a hard day, you say you had a worse day.

MAX: No I don't.

ANITA: Yes you do. You do that with everything. If I say my leg hurts, you say your knee and your elbow hurts.

MAX: Well, what I'm saying is that I can relate to your pain because I'm feeling some pain right now myself.

ANITA: You don't say that as a way to outdo me?

MAX: No.

ANITA: 'Cause it's like, I say, "Oh, I had a really hard day." And you say, "Well you should have my job. You could never handle doing what I do everyday." I don't think that's being sympathetic.

MAX: I don't say that when you say you had a really hard day.

ANITA: Yes you do.

Anita and Max certainly take a different approach to squabbling than do Bert and Betty. If you were a fly on the wall of their house you would hear a lot of *Coke* vs. *Pepsi* bickering: Who is a better cook? Is the drive from New York to Boston four hours or five? Whose mother is a bigger snoop? The content of their arguments is so minor, it's hard to imagine a couple like Bert and Betty wasting time on it. How can people like Max and Anita who seem to thrive on skirmishes live happily together? The truth is that not every couple who fights this frequently has a stable marriage. But we call those who do *volatile*. Such couples fight on a grand scale and have an even grander time making up. An uninvolved or withdrawn partner does not exist in a volatile marriage. These relationships are marked by a high level of engagement during discussions.

As you can see from the above dialogue, volatile couples like Max and Anita have little interest in hearing each other's point of view in the heat of argument—and I do mean heat! In essence, volatile couples simply skip the validator's first phase of discussing a delicate issue: they don't try to understand and empathize with their partner. Instead, they jump right into part two: trying to persuade. While validators tend to spend little time in the persuasion mode, for volatile couples, winning is what it's all about. That's why Anita and Max's discussion is littered with "yes you do," and "no I don't" rather than "mm-hmm" and "I see."

Here's how another volatile couple we studied "discussed" their differences over financial matters:

> REBECCA: I'm worried that we're not saving enough money. We seem to live hand to mouth.
>
> JOHN: I don't agree. We do not have a problem with finances. You're wrong.
>
> REBECCA: No, you're wrong. I would feel more secure if we had some savings.

For the sake of contrast, let me reconstruct the above dialogue to show how a validating couple might discuss the same issue:

> WIFE: I'm worried that we're not saving enough money. We seem to live hand to mouth.

HUSBAND: Uh huh. So you'd like to save more. Well I don't think we have a problem with finances.

WIFE: I see.

HUSBAND: I think you're wrong about our finances.

WIFE: Um hmm. I just would feel more secure if we had some savings.

HUSBAND: I see.

And I'm sure *you* see the difference too. While arguing à la John and Rebecca or Max and Anita may seem like a sure route to marital disaster, my research has found otherwise. It turns out that these couples' volcanic arguments are just a small part of an otherwise warm and loving marriage. The passion and relish with which they fight seems to fuel their positive interactions even more. Not only do they express more anger but they laugh and are more affectionate than the average validating couple. They express more negative *and* more positive emotions. These couples certainly do not find making up hard to do—they are masters at it. As intense as their battles may be, their good times are that much better.

Despite the vitriol, volatile couples are able to move to phase three: resolving their differences. For example, Max and Anita were able to navigate their way through the flashpoint in their marriage they discussed above—her belief that he always tries to outdo her complaints rather than be sympathetic. Max says he thinks Anita misinterprets his comments—that he is being supportive, but she doesn't hear it. She says it is his responsibility to express himself in a way that she will understand. He rejects the notion that this is solely his obligation:

MAX: Well, I don't think I should have to carry all the responsibility for whether we're getting along or not.

ANITA: How else is it gonna work?

MAX: If something I say bothers you, you should say to me: "Is this really what you're saying?" before you get emotionally involved.

ANITA: But I'm automatically going to have an emotional reaction to what you say!

MAX: (*Laughs*) But usually it's an emotion about something I *didn't* say. Sometimes you interpret what I say to be something like your dad would say, so you have a pat reaction that's not accurate to what *I've* actually said.

ANITA: So you think I should repeat what you said back to you.

MAX: Well, not always. But when you do repeat it, if I tell you that's *not* what I meant I want you to believe me.

ANITA: All right.

MAX: That's what I'd like.

ANITA: Okay.

MAX: I think that's the problem most of the time for me.

ANITA: That I don't believe you?

MAX: You just, yeah, stay with your biased, misconstrued reaction.

ANITA: Okay.

Just as validators tend to have certain qualities in common, volatile-like couples also share psychological characteristics. More than the other types, they see themselves as equals. They are independent sorts who believe that marriage should emphasize and strengthen individuality. While validating couples tend to finish each other's sentences, volatiles are more likely to interrupt each other with questions. At home they tend to have separate personal spaces and respect each other's privacy. They both consider themselves analytical. He also sees himself as nurturing; she as expressive. Indeed, they are very open with each other about their feelings—both positive and negative. The ease with which they disclose their innermost thoughts and emotions fuels both their battles and their romance. These marriages tend to be passionate and exciting, as if the marital punch has been spiked with danger.

Perhaps even more than the validating style, a volatile marriage has plenty of potential pitfalls. If the couple loses sight of the boundaries, they could slide from the stability of a volatile marriage into a style far more likely to destroy their bond. The overall danger is that their constant quarreling and bickering will consume the marriage, overwhelming their happy times together. If this occurs, even violence is possible in extreme cases. Of course, at that point we would no longer consider them to have a volatile marriage, but a highly unstable one.

Volatile couples seem to enjoy playfully teasing one another, but this brand of humor is also risky. Sometimes the playful teasing can hit a tender area and inadvertently lead to hurt feelings.

Also, because volatile couples tend to believe strongly that honesty in all matters is very important in a marriage, they censor very few of their thoughts. Their relentless commitment to honesty at whatever cost can be exhilarating and brave, but it can also be terrifying since it leaves no hurt unstated. It's easy to see how some hurts could arise that are difficult to heal and that therefore endanger the high levels of positivity that keep their marriage afloat. One exchange we video-taped of a volatile couple, Tom and Judy, showed how dangerously close to the edge this penchant for openness and self-disclosure can take a couple. In the course of discussing their sexual relationship, judy suddenly confessed, "Sometimes I think I could have sex with a perfect stranger . . . and just have no strings attached to it. That would be enjoyable. Because [between us] there are a whole lot of other things that get in the way, if I'm a little peeved with you about something."

This led Tom, a professor, to recall earlier in their marriage when he spent time "admiring the fit of those jeans" on women walking by him on campus. He tells Judy, "I remember that there were periods when I felt that way, and we'd get into a fight or something and one of us would say something like, 'if you're going to be that way about it, then we'll have to separate,' or something like that."

Suddenly, through their confessions the couple find themselves discussing the issue of breaking up. Now, Tom says he would "entertain the possibility" again in light of his wife's admission, but decides, "I don't like the feeling."

Judy agrees, "Oh freedom sounds good, but there are other aspects that are just too unsettling." Although these concluding comments restate their commitment to one another, there is a tentativeness to this affirmation of togetherness—a result of taking the confessions too far. At the end of the discussion they display an uneasiness that wasn't present when they first sat down.

The goal for volatile couples like Tom and Judy is to keep steady amidst the high winds of their passion. That can require quite a balancing act considering the frequent storms these couples subject themselves to. But as long as they hold on tight, I think they are likely to experience many years of joy and positive intensity.

JOE AND SHEILA: AVOIDANT

Moving from a volatile to an avoidant style marriage is like leaving the tumult of a hurricane for the placid waters of a summer lake. Not much seems to happen between husband and wife in this type of marriage. A more accurate name for them is probably *conflict minimizers* because they make light of their differences rather than resolving them. Like Joe and Sheila, these couples will claim that they have disagreements, but when you actually explore what they mean by *conflict* you realize that they conspire to dodge and hedge. We've seen that validators listen to each other's point of view before trying to persuade, while volatile couples jump right in, advocating for their opinion. But when avoidant couples air their differences very little gets settled. The phrase that comes up time and again when you speak with these couples about their marriage is that they end their friction by "agreeing to disagree." By this they usually mean that they avoid discussions they know will result in a deadlock.

Consider Sheila and Joe. In my view, their major conflict was a common—and potentially calamitous—one for a marriage. Namely, he wanted to have sex far more frequently than she did. She didn't enjoy sex with him, she said, because he was not as affectionate as she wanted at other times. He agreed that this was a problem and attributed it to his stress at work. Over time, she responded by becoming detached when they made love. It's not hard to imagine a conflict of this magnitude having serious consequences for a marriage. Yet, from their conversation it was clear that Sheila and Joe considered the issued "resolved":

INTERVIEWER: How do you each feel? Are you comfortable? Is it frustrating?

JOE: No, it's more of an ideological dispute in some ways than frustrating emotionally or physically.

SHEILA: I think I've come to feeling resigned about it. It's one thing I'm pretty sure is just not gonna be any different for us. . . . Sometimes I think we don't talk about things that we probably should, or that would be better if we did.

JOE: Well, you know, neither of us come from families that have very much physical contact.

SHEILA: We kids always did with my mother.

JOE: Well, we never did.

SHEILA: I don't know. It doesn't bother me. I mean, people make a big deal about having sex, sexual compatibility, and so on, but I think in the long run it's probably more important that we have our other compatibilities.

JOE: Yeah.

SHEILA: If our sex life was wonderful and we disagreed about everything else, we'd probably be considering divorce.

Though it is clear that Joe and Sheila disagreed on what frequency of physical contact felt right to them, neither attempted to persuade the other. Nor did they reach a compromise. They just concluded jointly that the conflict wasn't a big enough deal to work through. Each person stated his or her case, and that was the end of it. They felt that the common ground and values they shared overwhelmed the disagreement, making the conflict unimportant.

In a sense, conversations like Joe and Sheila's are standoffs. They reach some understanding that they disagree but do not explore the precise emotional nature of their differences. In these relationships, solving a problem usually means ignoring the difference, one partner agreeing to act more like the other (for example, if there is a dispute over disciplining children), or most often just letting time take its course. And yet, if you ask these couples whether they ever argue, many will readily say they do. And in a sense their reply is accurate: they do air their conflicts, but they follow up with only minimum attempts to convince each other of their point. They resolve their issues by avoiding or minimizing them.

Rather than resolve conflicts, avoidant couples appeal to their basic shared philosophy of marriage. They reaffirm what they love and value in the marriage, accentuate the positive, and accept the rest. In this way, they often end an unresolved discussion still feeling good about one another.

This type of successful coupling flies in the face of conventional wisdom that links marital stability to skillful "talking things out." So it seems a marriage *can* work even if a couple does not resolve their disputes. In contrast to the validating style, an avoidant style leads to a different sense of "we-ness":—it's as if the couple knows their bond is so strong they can overlook their disagreements. Yet there is a low level of companionship and sharing in the marriage. They value separateness and maintain autonomy in their use of space. These couples tend to live calm, pleasant lives. Though they display little of the intense passion of a volatile couple and less even than a validating couple, they face little of the risk that comes from testing their marriage as the other two types do.

One potentially problematic quality of the avoidant style, however, is that it leaves husband and wife very unschooled in how to address a conflict should they someday be forced to do so. If an issue develops that is too overwhelming to be handled through "agreeing to disagree," their marriage could end up like a fish washed up on shore, flailing about outside of its element. The result could be that negativity overwhelms their interaction and the marriage falls apart.

Another hazard of this type of marriage is that it can become lonely. These marriages are marked by a low degree of introspection or psychological sophistication. As a consequence, husband and/or wife may eventually feel that the other doesn't really know or understand them. This can occur when neither spouse is deeply aware of the real emotional bases of their upsets. In essence, they keep missing each other. If this becomes extreme, an avoidant marriage can get off course.

One couple we studied, Bill and Jane, are prime examples of this lack of introspection during arguments, although they remain happily married. The major source of strife in their marriage at the time they were interviewed was the hassle involved in building a new house. Jane's father was financing the project—and insisting on controlling even minor details of the construction. He was on the site regularly, informing the construction crew that he didn't think a light was needed over the kitchen counter, and so on. To an outside observer it was pretty obvious that the main source of tension between Jane and Bill was his resentment of her father's excessive involvement in the project and Jane's sense of divided loyalty between her husband and father. But in their arguments, neither Bill nor Jane ever raised either of these issues! Their exchanges didn't contain a single comment like, "I feel caught between you and my Dad," or, "I wish your Dad would just let us do it our way." Instead, they picked smaller, "safer" arguments such as whether a newspaper had advertised a paint sale at a local store, or whether Bill had talked to a workman on a particular day. These conflicts were easily resolved, leaving the couple with a renewed sense of unity, although they never actually addressed their underlying problem.

Clearly, though, there are drawbacks to an avoidant marriage just as there are to a volatile or validating one. It may well be that these different types of couples could glean a lot from each other's approach—for example, the volatile couple learning to ignore some conflicts and the avoidant one learning how to compromise. No matter how well suited husband and wife are, they may still need to work on their union to keep the balance intact and the love alive. (You'll find specific advice on enhancing these three marriage styles in chapter 7.) But the prognosis for these types of marriages is quite positive. In fact, I believe a successful marriage generally evolves into one of these three types—they are each healthy adaptations to living intimately with another human being.

The three types of stable couples will each say that they discuss feelings fully in their marriage and resolve issues. But they differ vastly on these dimensions and on what feels like a satisfying resolution. What is far more important than actually solving the issue or problem is feeling good about the interaction itself, and each of these types of couples has its own way to do that. Here, for example, is how each kind of couple might deal with the identical problem. First, the validating couple:

HUSBAND: You've never been to church with me. I wish you'd come some time.

WIFE: You know I don't believe in organized religion.

HUSBAND: I'm not asking you to believe.

WIFE: What then?

HUSBAND: I get lonely without you.

WIFE: You're saying you miss me?

HUSBAND: Yeah, I am.

WIFE: You're not trying to convert?

HUSBAND: Maybe a little, but no. I just wish we'd be together as a family.

WIFE: I kind of miss you too on Sunday morning.

HUSBAND: I also think it's good for the kids.

WIFE: I agree.

HUSBAND: What about coming some time?

WIFE: No pressure?

HUSBAND: No pressure.

WIFE: I'll think about it.

HUSBAND: Fair enough.

Here's how the conversation about church might have sounded if a volatile couple had been having it:

HUSBAND: You've never been to church with me. I wish you'd come some time.

WIFE: You know I don't believe in organized religion.

HUSBAND: I want to get Jason baptized.

WIFE: (*Raising her voice*) Why? So he doesn't go to purgatory for original sin if he dies?

HUSBAND: Because I feel it says that he has a spiritual life, that he's part of a religious community.

WIFE: You got that from the priest.

HUSBAND: Well, he said it quite well.

WIFE: (*Sarcastically*) You're a lawyer and you can't put it in your own words?

HUSBAND: God's got too good a case.

WIFE: (*Laughs*) Yeah, we don't want to fight God.

HUSBAND: (*Laughs*) Since you don't believe in any of it, why not go along with what I want?

This is what the conversation about going to church might have sounded like if the couple were conflict avoiders:

HUSBAND: You've never been to church with me.

WIFE: Um-hmm, that's true.

HUSBAND: I wish you'd come some time.

WIFE: I prefer the time alone.

HUSBAND: Well, okay. It's not real important to me actually.

WIFE: We have a lot else going for us, you know.

HUSBAND: Oh I think ours is a great marriage. Yeah, my sister and Jeff go all the time and they fight like cats and dogs. Religion doesn't do much for them. I just thought I'd ask.

WIFE: I'm glad you brought it up. But you know I could put in the time on our remodeling. We're so close to getting started with the plans.

HUSBAND: That'd be more important, really, than your going with me to church. Go ahead.

WIFE: You don't mind?

HUSBAND: No. It's no big deal. It's not an issue.

WIFE: I'll come to the picnics.

HUSBAND: Fine. That'd be fine.

WIFE: You don't mind?

HUSBAND: Not really.

WIFE: Good.

NEGOTIATING A TYPE OF STABLE MARRIAGE

Every couple probably goes through a negotiation starting early in their relationship for what style they will have. Partners often differ in the level of emotional intensity they are most comfortable with, and in their preferred way of handling emotional strife. It may seem unlikely that someone who would be most comfortable in an avoidant marriage would select someone who would be most comfortable in a volatile marriage, but I have seen it happen. Opposites do attract, at least sometimes. For example, I know a very emotionally controlled man who married a very expressive woman. She loved his stability and he loved her fire. After a while, though, he wished that she would be less explosive, more rational, and show more emotional control, and she wished he would be more spontaneous, responsive, and expressive. He wanted more privacy, psychological space, and autonomy than she found comfortable. They had trouble negotiating a marital style with which they could each live.

This negotiation is a hard task, but essential if you are to find stability. I think it may be possible to borrow from each marital style and create a viable mixed style. Being aware of the styles available to you may help in finding your own balance. But so long as you and your partner desire different types of marriage you will be at special risk for the emergence of what I call "The Four Horsemen of the Apocalypse" in your marriage. And that is the topic of the next chapter.

SELF-TEST: YOUR MARITAL TYPE

My research classifies stable couples into three types based on how they act toward each other: how expressive they are emotionally and the amount and timing of their attempts to persuade each other during conflict. But couples who fall into one of the three stable types of marriages differ not only in their actions but also in the thoughts and attitudes with which they feel comfortable. The questionnaire below will help you explore this less tangible dimension of your marriage. It asks about both the way your marriage is now, and your opinions or preferences for how you think a marriage should be.

Whatever the current status of your marriage, it can help to have a sense of which type of relationship would ideally work best for you. Please think of these items only as a general guide. Your scores on this questionnaire may indicate that the optimum kind of marriage for you may be a hybrid rather than one of these three basic types. That's okay. Probably the best way to think of this test is as a story you tell yourself about what aspects of these three types appeal to you. Think of them as primary colors that you can use to form your own palette.

I want you to take the following test, and also have your partner take it. If your partner is unable or unwilling to take the test, then you can take it twice—first answering for yourself, then again as you would imagine your partner would answer. Comparing your scores may show you the differences or similarities in how you perceive your marriage or the direction you'd like it to take. And that can be the basis for discussing what accommodations you might make to find your own most agreeable ways to handle conflicts (see chapter 8 for more ideas on how to work this out).

Directions: Answer "yes" or "no" to each statement below depending on how much you generally agree with it.

• *Part I* •
IS THE CONFLICT AVOIDER STYLE OF MARRIAGE
RIGHT FOR YOU?

1. I will often hide my feelings to avoid hurting my spouse.
YOU: Yes   No   YOUR PARTNER: Yes   No

2. When we disagree, I don't believe there is much point in analyzing our feelings and motivations.
YOU: Yes   No   YOUR PARTNER: Yes   No

3. When we disagree, we often solve the problem by going back to our basic beliefs about the different roles of men and women in marriage.
YOU: Yes   No   YOUR PARTNER: Yes   No

4. We have a lot of separate friends.
YOU: Yes   No   YOUR PARTNER: Yes   No

5. It is important to attend a church or synagogue regularly.
YOU: Yes   No   YOUR PARTNER: Yes   No

6. Many marital conflicts are solved just through the passing of time.
You: Yes   No   Your Partner: Yes   No

7. We each do a lot of things on our own.
You: Yes   No   Your Partner: Yes   No

8. During a marital conflict, there is not much to be gained from figuring out what is happening on a psychological level.
You: Yes   No   Your Partner: Yes   No

9. Our religious values give us a clear sense of life's purposes.
You: Yes   No   Your Partner: Yes   No

10. When I'm moody I prefer to be left alone until I get over it.
You: Yes   No   Your Partner: Yes   No

11. I don't feel very comfortable with strong displays of negative emotion in my marriage.
You: Yes   No   Your Partner: Yes   No

12. We turn to our basic religious or cultural values for guidance when resolving conflicts.
You: Yes   No   Your Partner: Yes   No

13. I just accept most of the things in my marriage that I can't change.
You: Yes   No   Your Partner: Yes   No

14. We often agree not to talk about things we disagree about.
You: Yes   No   Your Partner: Yes   No

15. In our marriage there is a fairly clear line between the husband's and wife's roles.
You: Yes   No   Your Partner: Yes   No

16. We just don't seem to disagree very much.
You: Yes   No   Your Partner: Yes   No

17. When we have some difference of opinion we often just drop the topic.
You: Yes   No   Your Partner: Yes   No

18. We hardly ever have much to argue about.
You: Yes   No   Your Partner: Yes   No

19. A lot of talking about disagreements often makes matters worse.
You: Yes   No   Your Partner: Yes   No

20. There are some personal areas in my life that I prefer not to discuss with my spouse.
You: Yes   No   Your Partner: Yes   No

21. There is not much point in trying to persuade my partner of my viewpoint.
You: Yes   No   YOUR PARTNER: Yes   No

22. There's not much to be gained by getting openly angry with my spouse.
You: Yes   No   YOUR PARTNER: Yes   No

23. Thinking positively solves a lot of marital issues.
You: Yes   No   YOUR PARTNER: Yes   No

24. In marriage it is usually best to stick to the traditional values about men and women.
You: Yes   No   YOUR PARTNER: Yes   No

25. I prefer to work out many of my negative feelings on my own.
You: Yes   No   YOUR PARTNER: Yes   No

26. Going over a lot of negative feelings in a marital discussion usually makes things worse.
You: Yes   No   YOUR PARTNER: Yes   No

27. If you just relax about problems, they have a way of working themselves out.
You: Yes   No   YOUR PARTNER: Yes   No

28. When we talk about our problems we find they just aren't that important in the overall picture of our marriage.
You: Yes   No   YOUR PARTNER: Yes   No

29. Men and women ought to have separate roles in a marriage.
You: Yes   No   YOUR PARTNER: Yes   No

Scoring: Total up the number of items you checked "Yes." If the number is greater than eight, you probably feel comfortable with a conflict-avoider marriage philosophy.

COMFORT WITH AN AVOIDER PHILOSOPHY (CHECKED EIGHT OR MORE YES)?

	YES	NO
You		
Your Partner		

• *Part II* •
ARE YOU COMFORTABLE WITH A VOLATILE
OR VALIDATOR STYLE OF MARRIAGE?

1. I think it's a good idea for my partner and me to have a lot of separate friends.
YOU: Yes   No   YOUR PARTNER: Yes   No

2. I believe in honestly confronting disagreements, whatever the issue.
YOU: Yes   No   YOUR PARTNER: Yes   No

3. We often do things separately.
YOU: Yes   No   YOUR PARTNER: Yes   No

4. The feeling of togetherness is very central to our marriage.
YOU: Yes   No   YOUR PARTNER: Yes   No

5. Marriage partners should be direct and honest no matter what the results.
YOU: Yes   No   YOUR PARTNER: Yes   No

6. I feel quite comfortable with a strong expression of negative feelings.
YOU: Yes   No   YOUR PARTNER: Yes   No

7. Sometimes I enjoy a good argument with my spouse.
YOU: Yes   No   YOUR PARTNER: Yes   No

8. The most important aspect of marriage is companionship.
YOU: Yes   No   YOUR PARTNER: Yes   No

9. Jealousy is sometimes an issue in our marriage.
YOU: Yes   No   YOUR PARTNER: Yes   No

10. It is important to be a separate individual in a marriage.
YOU: Yes   No   YOUR PARTNER: Yes   No

11. I think we should argue but only about important issues.
YOU: Yes   No   YOUR PARTNER: Yes   No

12. We often will eat separately.
YOU: Yes   No   YOUR PARTNER: Yes   No

13. Our marriage is based on being one another's best friend.
YOU: Yes   No   YOUR PARTNER: Yes   No

14. I enjoy trying to persuade my spouse when we have a disagreement.
YOU: Yes   No   YOUR PARTNER: Yes   No

15. The religious and other beliefs we share are basic to our marriage.
YOU: Yes   No   YOUR PARTNER: Yes   No

16. I believe in keeping our marriage very romantic.
You: Yes   No   Your Partner: Yes   No

17. We often look back at our photo albums together.
You: Yes   No   Your Partner: Yes   No

18. We cultivate a sense of we-ness in our marriage.
You: Yes   No   Your Partner: Yes   No

19. We share all things personal and emotional in our marriage.
You: Yes   No   Your Partner: Yes   No

20. All the spaces in our home are shared spaces.
You: Yes   No   Your Partner: Yes   No

21. I would never take a separate vacation from my spouse.
You: Yes   No   Your Partner: Yes   No

22. At times I enjoy expressing anger.
You: Yes   No   Your Partner: Yes   No

23. I believe it is important to fight even about small matters.
You: Yes   No   Your Partner: Yes   No

24. I enjoy working out our values through thorough arguments.
You: Yes   No   Your Partner: Yes   No

25. There is nothing personal that I do not share with my spouse.
You: Yes   No   Your Partner: Yes   No

26. I am comfortable only with a moderate amount of emotional expression.
You: Yes   No   Your Partner: Yes   No

27. It is essential to have a strong sense of togetherness in marriage.
You: Yes   No   Your Partner: Yes   No

28. Keeping a certain amount of distance in a marriage helps the romance.
You: Yes   No   Your Partner: Yes   No

29. A strong sense of traditional values is good for a marriage.
You: Yes   No   Your Partner: Yes   No

30. There are few issues in a marriage worth arguing about.
You: Yes   No   Your Partner: Yes   No

Scoring: In the *Validator* and *Volatile* columns below, put a check next to the number of each question you answered "yes" to above. Next, separately add up all the check marks in each column. Divide each sum by 15. This will give you percentage scores for your comfort level with each style. For example, you may wind up with a 53 percent score on the *Volatile* scale and an 80 percent score on the *Validator* scale. This suggests that you are mostly comfortable with a validator philosophy of marriage, although there are elements of the volatile type with which you are also comfortable.

VOLATILE	VALIDATOR
1	4
2	8
3	11
5	13
6	15
7	17
9	18
10	19
12	20
14	21
16	25
22	26
23	27
24	29
28	30

Volatile Total/15 = Volatile %
Validator Total/15 = Validator %

	VOLATILE		VALIDATOR	
	YES	NO	YES	NO
You				
Your Partner				

THE MAGIC RATIO: ACCENTUATE THE POSITIVE; DON'T ELIMINATE THE NEGATIVE

By now you may be wondering how these three very different types of marriages can be equally successful, or how couples with such clear difficulties, differences, or apparent inadequacies can stay happily together. The answer is that happiness isn't found in a particular style of fighting or making up. Rather, our research suggests that what really separates contented couples from those in deep marital misery is a healthy balance between their positive and negative feelings and actions toward each other. For example, I mentioned that volatile couples stick together by *balancing* their frequent arguments with a lot of love and passion. But by balance I do not mean a fifty-fifty equilibrium. As part of our research we carefully charted the amount of time couples spent fighting versus interacting positively—touching, smiling, paying compliments, laughing, etc. Across the board we found there was a very specific ratio that exists between the amount of positivity and negativity in a stable marriage, whether it is marked by validation, volatility, or conflict avoidance.

That magic ratio is 5 *to* 1. In other words, as long as there is five times as much positive feeling and interaction between husband and wife as there is negative, we found the marriage was likely to be stable. It was based on this ratio that we were able to predict whether couples were likely to divorce: in very unhappy couples, there tended to be more negative than positive interaction.

One way to think of a stable couple is as a stereo system in which five times as much power is emitted from the positive loudspeaker as from the negative one. No matter what the particular couple's volume level, the balance between their positive and negative speakers remains roughly the same. High-volume volatile couples may yell and scream a lot, but they spend five times as much of their marriage being loving and making up. Validators have a moderate amount of tension and an immoderate level of fun, loving, and warmth. Quieter, avoidant couples may not display as much passion as the other types, but they display far less criticism and contempt as well—the ratio is still 5 to 1.

The three successful styles of marriage are equally successful adaptations that allow very different kinds of couples to maintain this crucial ratio over time. In other words, these three styles may be universal ways of preserving this important balance (or rather, *imbal-ance* in favor of the positive scale). Whether a couple settles into a validating, volatile, or avoidant marriage may depend on their partic-ular temperaments, backgrounds, and personalities.

You can think of the 5-to-1 ratio as akin to the pH of soil, the balance between acidity and alkalinity that is crucial to fertility. Your marriage needs much more positivity than negativity to nourish your love. Without it, your relationship is in danger of withering and dying, just like a fragile vine that is planted in soil that is too acidic, too sandy, or too dry. In that 5-to-1 ratio, positivity acts as a nutrient, nurturing the affection and joy that are crucial if your love is to weather the rough spots.

While I found that this magic ratio of 5-to-1 held across all three stable types, the picture was very different for couples who were heading for a breakup: they showed slightly more negative than positive acts. This difference in the two ratios meant that in their moment-to-moment interactions husbands and wives in each of the three stable kinds of marriages were balancing their negativity with a whopping amount of positivity, whereas those couples who were heading for divorce were doing far too little on the positive side to compensate for the growing negativity between them. For those in the low-key avoidant marriages, less positivity is needed, because less negativity is expressed. But for those in the passionate, high-volatility matches, a very high level of positivity is demanded to make up for all the negativity in the air.

What were the negative emotions? You will read all about them in this book, particularly criticism and contempt, defensiveness and withdrawal, loneliness and isolation. But the list does not include anger! When I started the research I assumed, like most researchers and clinicians, that anger was destructive if there was "too much" of it. But when I looked at what predicted divorce or separation, I found that anger only has negative effects in marriage if it is expressed along with criticism or contempt, or if it is defensive.

What exactly were these stable couples doing with each other to maintain a positive balance for their negative emotions? For one thing, by and large—even in the volatile couples—they were far less negative than the couples who eventually split up. When they brought up disagreements, they were less extreme in expressing feelings like anger or frustration. They complained and got angry, to be sure, but they were less critical of their spouse, less defensive, less contemptuous, and they were engaged—not disapproving—listeners. Even the men in conflict-avoiding marriages, who were not very engaged as listeners, were very positive when it became their turn to speak; their withdrawal as listeners was not the sullen type that leads to being a defensive speaker.

What was even more striking was the many ways, large and small, that stable couples showed their positivity. It translates into a useful list of ways to put more weight on the positive side of the equation in your marriage. For example:

Show interest. Be actively interested in what your partner is saying. Your wife, for example, complains about an employee who is irresponsible and makes her miss her bus. You say, with feeling and energy, "He really did that? I can't believe he came late again and you had to stay and miss your bus!" But interest can be signaled more subtly, simply by showing you are truly listening and involved—timely "uh-huhs," nods, and looking your spouse in the eye while she talks.

Be affectionate. You can show affection in low-key, subtle ways simply through quiet acts of tenderness: touching or holding hands while you watch TV, intertwining your feet while you read the Sunday paper together. Such physical affection has a contented, dreamy quality, like sitting in front of the fire and enjoying its warmth together. There need be nothing said. More actively, little things you say or do can remind your partner of your affection: a reminiscence of a happy time together, of an expression of solidarity ("This is our problem, not just yours; we're in this together"), doing something thoughtful—or simply offering to do it. Affection is implicit any time the two of you are having a really good time together. And, of course, there are the most obvious expressions of affection, voicing your feelings of love, or romantic passion.

Show you care. Small acts of thoughtfulness are a powerful way to boost the positivity in your marriage. Some examples: You are shopping and you pass a florist; you buy your wife some flowers she'd like. Or you're in the grocery store and you think of getting your husband's favorite ice cream. Or you just take a few minutes during your busy day and think about what your partner is facing today; for example, "Right now she is about to run a meeting about staff conflicts and she is real worried about how it will go because of that domineering person on her staff." And you call up to check in, wish her well, see how things are going.

Be appreciative. You put positive energy into the marriage simply through appreciating it—thinking about and remembering positive moments from your past, thinking fondly about your partner, and so on. Stoking these positive memories and thoughts is a counterbalance to those moments when you may get carried away by negativity and find it hard to recall anything good about your marriage. Agreeing with your partner's ideas, suggestions, or solutions is another form of appreciation. And every time you let your partner know that you realize you've got a good thing—say, by giving a compliment or expressing pride in your partner—you strengthen the bond between you.

Show your concern. Whenever your partner tells you about something distressing or troubling, express your concern. Be supportive when your partner is blue or worried: "Your job is really getting you down and I'm bothered by that. Let's talk it over." Apologies help; say your partner was upset by something you said, and has turned on you with hurt and anger—it makes a big difference if you're able to say, "I'm really sorry that what I said hurt your feelings" instead of becoming defensive about it and trying to justify your remark.

Be empathic. Empathy, showing your partner an emotional resonance, is a potent form of affection. You can show that you really understand and feel what your partner is feeling just through an expression on your face that matches your partner's. But empathy can't be faked. If you say, "I know how you feel," without it really being true, your partner will sense that false emotional note. More empathic is saying something that shows understanding, like, "Oh, that really hurt when she said that, didn't it?"

Be accepting. Even if your partner is saying something you don't agree with, let your partner know what he or she is saying makes sense and is important—that you respect it. This acceptance can be tacit, such as assenting with a "yeah" while your partner is talking, which shows you are listening, want to hear more, and that what's being said makes some sense to you; it also shows that you accept the feelings being expressed. Summarizing your partner's point of view during a spat is another form of acceptance, even if you still disagree.

Joke around. Playful teasing, wittiness, silliness, and just having an uproarious time together is especially nourishing. If you, like most couples, have private jokes that only you share, such joking is a way not only to have fun but is also a statement of the intimate and exclusive bond between you. But if your spouse does not find your teasing, hostile, or sarcastic jokes funny, beware: that is an act of belligerence, not humor.

Share your joy. When you're feeling delighted, excited, or just having a really good time, let your partner know it.

Of course, you probably do much or most of this spontaneously. But it may be helpful to remember that these are the marks that keep your marriage on the positive side of that 5-to-1 ratio. And while all of this comes naturally when things are good between you, an intentional effort during rocky periods can help you get back to a more positive balance.

Like the Second Law of Thermodynamics, which says that in closed energy systems things tend to run down and get less orderly, the same seems to be true of closed relationships like marriages. My guess is that if you do nothing to make things get better in your marriage but do not do anything wrong, the marriage will still tend to get worse over time. To maintain a balanced emotional ecology you need to make an effort—think about your spouse during the day, think about how to make a good thing even better, and act.

BASIC MARITAL NUTRIENTS: LOVE AND RESPECT

In our study of long-term marriages we recruited couples from a wide range of backgrounds who had been married twenty to forty years to the same partner. Despite the wide differences in occupations, lifestyles, and the details of their day-to-day lives, I sense a remarkable similarity in the tone of their conversations. No matter what style of marriage they have adopted, their discussions, for the most part, are carried along by a strong undercurrent of two basic ingredients: love and respect.

These are the direct opposite of—and antidote for—contempt,

perhaps the most corrosive force in marriage. But all the ways partners show each other love and respect also ensure that the positive-to-negative ratio of a marriage will be heavily tilted to the positive side.

The abundance of love and respect in these long-term marriages is evident everywhere. Watching the tapes, I see a great deal of affection exchanged through gestures, eye contact, and facial expressions. During the silent "rest periods" between each of Mike and Dorothy's conversations, for example, we spy Dorothy catching Mike's eye and flirting with him in what appears to be some secret sign language. Later on, he brags shamelessly to the interviewer about Dorothy's talent at crafts and gardening. This is a common occurrence among partners from these long-term marriages. Many jump at the chance to tell the interviewer about their partner's skills and achievements. They also express genuine interest in the details of each other's lives. When conflicts arise, each gives consideration to the other's point of view.

One couple who met as peace activists in Berkeley in the 1960s, for example, appear to get a big kick out of their heated debate over free speech, censorship, and civil liberties. They've been hashing out the same issues for more than two decades, gaining esteem in one another's eyes as their arguments grow sharper. Later on, this same couple reflects aloud on how proud they are of their children, and how nice it is just to feel each other's toes under the covers.

Such masters of marital harmony express lots of empathy and sympathy for one another. When illness strikes one partner, the other is there with just the right amount of nurturing and support. They also offer one another refuge from the tedium and indignities of daily life. They're likely to say things like, "I'm really sorry that the computer ate your sales report," or, "Your boss obviously underestimates your hidden talent."

What about your marriage? Do you and your spouse take the opportunity to show your love and respect on a regular basis? How are these feelings expressed in your relationship? Here is a quick test to help you to identify your strengths and weaknesses.

• Part III •

SELF-TEST:
IS THERE ENOUGH LOVE AND RESPECT
IN YOUR MARRIAGE?

Answer "yes" or "no" to each of the following statements, depending on whether you mostly agree or disagree. As before, take the test on behalf of your partner also, if necessary.

1. My spouse seeks out my opinions.
YOU: Yes   No   YOUR PARTNER: Yes   No

2. My spouse cares about my feelings.
YOU: Yes   No   YOUR PARTNER: Yes   No

3. I don't feel ignored very often.
YOU: Yes   No   YOUR PARTNER: Yes   No

4. We touch each other a lot.
YOU: Yes   No   YOUR PARTNER: Yes   No

5. We listen to each other.
YOU: Yes   No   YOUR PARTNER: Yes   No

6. We respect each other's ideas.
YOU: Yes   No   YOUR PARTNER: Yes   No

7. We are affectionate toward one another.
YOU: Yes   No   YOUR PARTNER: Yes   No

8. I feel that my partner takes good care of me.
YOU: Yes   No   YOUR PARTNER: Yes   No

9. What I say counts.
YOU: Yes   No   YOUR PARTNER: Yes   No

10. I am important in our decisions.
YOU: Yes   No   YOUR PARTNER: Yes   No

11. There's lots of love in our marriage.
YOU: Yes   No   YOUR PARTNER: Yes   No

12. We are genuinely interested in one another.
YOU: Yes   No   YOUR PARTNER: Yes   No

13. I just love spending time with my partner.
YOU: Yes   No   YOUR PARTNER: Yes   No

14. We are very good friends.
YOU: Yes   No   YOUR PARTNER: Yes   No

15. Even during rough times, we can be empathetic.
You: Yes   No   YOUR PARTNER: Yes   No

16. My spouse is considerate of my viewpoint.
You: Yes   No   YOUR PARTNER: Yes   No

17. My spouse finds me physically attractive.
You: Yes   No   YOUR PARTNER: Yes   No

18. My partner expresses warmth toward me.
You: Yes   No   YOUR PARTNER: Yes   No

19. I feel included in my partner's life.
You: Yes   No   YOUR PARTNER: Yes   No

20. My spouse admires me.
You: Yes   No   YOUR PARTNER: Yes   No

Scoring: If you checked "yes" to fewer than seven items, then it is likely you are not feeling adequately loved and respected in your marriage. You need to be far more active and creative in adding affection to your relationship.

THE ECOLOGY OF MARRIAGE

The balance between negativity and positivity seems to be the key dynamic in what amounts to the emotional ecology of every marriage. Like the atmosphere or oceans, the health of an intimate relationship is an ecosystem of sorts, one where there are crucial rates of emotional exchange. If these rates are in balance, love thrives; when they get too far out of balance, then the love between a couple can start to wither and die, like an endangered species starved of its basic nutrients.

There seems to be some kind of thermostat operating in healthy marriages that regulates the balance between positivity and negativity, preserving a sound emotional ecology. It's as if, for example, when partners in a stable marriage get contemptuous, they correct it with lots of positivity—not necessarily right away, but sometime soon.

The balance also implies a strange thing, something you, like me, may find hard to believe at first: that certain kinds of *negativity* may actually have some *positive* function in marriages. For example, some degree of negativity may help keep sexual passion in a marriage. Many couples have experienced the aphrodisiacal effect of a good fight—once it's time to make up. Perhaps for such couples certain kinds of negativity act like fuel that reignites desire. Its role in a healthy marriage may be to spur a cycle of closeness and distance that can renew love and affection. "Off" times allow couples to become reacquainted periodically and heighten their love. Too much of it, of course, can consume a marriage forever.

A friend once told me a story of a fight he had with his wife in which she felt that he had ignored her when they had house guests. She was very upset, but she would not discuss her feelings. For the first time in years she refused to talk to him. He was very distressed by all this, but gradually he accepted it and they both became silent, angry, recriminating, and sullen. Although they stayed distantly polite, this distance grew and grew over time. They still slept in the same bed but they avoided touching each other.

One day he saw his wife dressing as they prepared to go out together to a special concert. The evening had been planned months in advance, the tickets to the concert were very expensive, and neither of them had any intention of not going. As he watched his wife dress for the evening and comb her long hair he was struck by her beauty in a way he hadn't experienced in years. He was hypnotized by her shining hair, and he fell in love with the look of pride and dignity she held in her aloofness from him.

As the evening proceeded they found that they both enjoyed the concert a great deal and they forgot themselves a little bit. Their hands met and the touch was as electric as when they had first become lovers. They looked deeply into one another's eyes and kissed. That night they made passionate love. Afterward they held each other, and in the morning everything was all right. It was better than all right—something had been renewed. My friend and I wondered if the fight was really about anything real at all, or if it was part of a dance of distance and closeness in a marriage that in some way serves to renew the courtship, or, at least, the attraction.

One of the first things to go in a marriage is politeness. In some ways this simply reflects increasing comfort. But it leads to taking one another for granted, and it can lead to rudeness. The difference between the conversation of spouses and people who are strangers is that the married couples are far less polite to each other than to the strangers. When paired with a stranger, even newlyweds accepted the other person's opinions more readily, disagreed less, and were more polite than they were with their partners. In a marriage there are delicate balances operating, and negativity and conflict may sometimes serve positive functions of renewal.

One intriguing question is why negativity is necessary at all for a marriage to survive. Why don't stable marriages have a positive-to-negative ratio that is more like 100 to 1? Wouldn't marriages work best if there were *no* disagreements? Our research suggests that in the short run this may be true. But for a marriage to have real staying power, couples need to air their differences, whether they resolve them in a volatile, validating, or minimizing style. For example, we found that couples who fought were less satisfied with their marriages than those who described their interactions as peaceful. But when we checked on these couples three years later, we found the situation had reversed. Those who did *not* fight earlier on were less likely to have maintained stable marriages than those who were more confrontational. The originally "happy" couples were more likely to be on the trajectory toward divorce, or even be divorced, than the others. In other words, what may lead to temporary misery in a marriage—disagreement and anger—may be healthy for it in the long run. Rather than being destructive, occasional anger can be a resource that helps the marriage improve over time.

Such findings have led to my belief that in the ecology of marriage a certain amount of negativity is required for the union to thrive. In the wild, it is usual for a species to have a predator that keeps its population in check and ensures the survival of the fittest. Antelopes, for example, are naturally preyed upon by lions. If there are too many lions in the environs, the antelope population will dwindle dangerously. Not enough lions and the antelope population becomes too large, causing it to die off from lack of food. Predators also play a clean-up role, weeding out the weakest members of a population so that the strongest ones, those most likely to spawn healthy offspring, are most likely to survive.

I think that in the marital ecosystem negativity is the predator. In a sense, it is the lion that preys on the positive interactions between husband and wife. Too much negativity and the marriage becomes doomed. But too little can be destructive as well. In the ecology of marriage, some degree of negative interaction keeps the union strong. A certain amount of conflict is necessary to help couples weed out actions and ways of dealing with each other that can harm the marriage in the long run. Even avoidant couples do air their conflicts—they just have an avoidant way of resolving them. I don't believe their marriages would be stable if they didn't talk over their complaints at all.

It's important to keep in mind that negativity comes in many different guises. A marriage can be harmed by too much of it or certain types of it. Namely, when negative energy includes great stubbornness, contempt, defensiveness, or withdrawal from interaction, the results on the marriage can be devastating. And when a couple fails to find the equilibrium of a stable marital style, then they are vulnerable to having those corrosive, negative forces eat away at their marriage. The next few chapters will help you gauge exactly which of these destructive patterns have begun to take hold in your marriage; the final chapters will tell you what to do about them to help your marriage stay healthy.

THREE

THE FOUR HORSEMEN OF THE APOCALYPSE: WARNING SIGNS

Although my work has introduced me to plenty of volatile couples like Anita and Max, whose passions have mostly added joy to their marriages, I've met too many others whose heated exchanges were not compensated for by humor or affection. If you listened to such couples argue, at first glance they might not sound much different from a volatile couple. But unlike volatile couples, they don't spend far more time laughing and joking, touching, caressing, *loving* each other than they do locking horns. Even more damaging, their frequent arguments are marked by toxic types of negativity such as contempt and defensiveness.

These are couples who have failed to find an equilibrium in one of the three stable types of marriage. Their emotional ecology is in trouble and their marriage is beginning to spin out of control. Such couples are trapped in one of two destructive, unbalanced types of unions my research has uncovered. These marriages offer snapshots of a marital meltdown in progress.

These unions, I found, are almost certain to end in divorce as the years go on. But they are a crucial object lesson if you want to be alert to the processes that can quietly begin to corrode your marriage.

In these highly troubled marriages you can see in bold highlights the specific ways in which even a contented couple can begin to slip away from each other. Every marriage demands an effort to keep it on the right track; there is a constant tension within the emotional ecology of every couple between the forces that hold you together and those that can tear you apart. Even if you and your spouse have arrived at a stable pattern, you should be alert to the early warning signs that tell you if you are beginning to get shunted toward a dead end.

This chapter and chapters 4 and 5 will help you assess your own marriage, and diagnose the specific signs, if any, of trouble. The last part of the book will tell you what to do to keep your marriage strong and healthy.

TWO PORTRAITS OF MARITAL MELTDOWN

The first kind of marriage in freefall toward destruction is what I call the hostile/engaged type. These couples argue often and hotly. Insults, name-calling, put-downs, sarcasm are all part of their repertoire. Here's a typical exchange between a hostile/engaged couple:

FRED: Did you pick up my dry cleaning?

INGRID: (*Mocking*) "Did you pick up my dry cleaning?" Pick up your own damn dry cleaning. What am I, your maid?

FRED: Hardly. If you were a maid, at least you'd know how to clean.

In some cases when a marriage becomes imbalanced, husband and wife may yell and abuse each other, but neither really listens to what the other is saying, nor do they look at each other very much. Such couples are quite detached and emotionally uninvolved, but they get into brief episodes of attack and defensiveness. Rather than hostile/engaged, these couples are what I call *hostile/detached*. You can see this style in the interaction between the unhappily married Molly and Dick:

MOLLY: Don't you think we get along a little better?

DICK: Yeah . . . but I get tired of hearing how hot it is.

MOLLY: Well, those are the things people talk about. I'm sorry.

DICK: Not just the weather. I don't want to listen unless it's pleasant. If there is something I don't enjoy, I don't wanna talk about it.

MOLLY: If you're not particularly enjoying yourself you just don't wanna talk.

DICK: Right. If it's not pleasant. I don't wanna talk about it if the subject isn't pleasant.

MOLLY: Yeah? You're the only family I've got, and damn it, if I have to keep all my problems to myself, I might as well live by myself.

How did Fred and Ingrid, and Molly and Dick get that way? For some reason, they were unable to move toward one of the three stabilizing adaptations to married life. Our research suggests that the farther afield you are from one of these three types, the more likely you are to veer onto the path that can lead from wedded bliss to marital disaster. It may be that these unfortunate marriages result when husband and wife are mismatched in the style of marriage they want. For example, a wife whose natural tendency is to be validating will choose her battle grounds carefully. She may feel overwhelmed by a volatile husband who is quick to make sparks fly over a wet dishrag left in the sink. Over time, their happy marriage may deteriorate into a hostile or hostile/detached one. Or, an avoidant wife may feel her marriage is put at risk each time her validating husband insists that they confront and resolve a conflict rather than sidestep it. Eventually, the ecological balance of such a marriage can go awry. Negativity, a marriage's major predator, can overgrow and eventually kill off the positive reasons husband and wife bonded in the first place.

The good news is that this needn't happen. If, after taking the self-test on page 51, you have concluded that your marriage does not fall neatly into one of the three successful adaptations, don't despair. You can still sustain a rewarding, happy coupling. However, such a marriage may be at higher risk of instability, unless when trouble strikes *you understand what is going wrong and why*. I think it is certainly possible to develop this sort of insight. In fact, much of our research has focused on mapping exactly how marriages go from good to bad to worse. We have been able to chart fairly specific sequences of reactivity and negative emotions that become increasingly destructive, building force and momentum as a marriage goes farther and farther down the wrong track. By knowing the warning signs and dangers of these cascades you have a far better chance of avoiding them or extricating your marriage if the downward roll has already begun. If you do so, I believe that eventually your marriage will end up resembling one of the three satisfying types that my research has linked to long-term happiness.

TUMBLING DOWN THE MARITAL RAPIDS

"All happy families are alike but an unhappy family is unhappy after its own fashion." So reads the opening sentence of *Anna Karenina* by Leo Tolstoy. Although often quoted, Tolstoy's view is woefully inaccurate. If you are in the middle of a troubled marriage it can seem that your predicament is not only unique but nearly impossible to sort out. But in fact unhappy marriages do resemble each other in important ways. True, each has its own personality and idiosyncracies, but they share one overriding similarity: they followed the same, *specific*, downward spiral before coming to a sad end. This spiral includes a distinct cascade of interactions, emotions, and attitudes that, step by step, brought these couples close to separation, divorce, or an unhappy, lonely life together. Rather than settling into one of the three stable marital styles, their relationships went into a freefall as they were consumed by negativity. By identifying this trajectory toward marital dissolution, my research team has been able to predict with remarkable accuracy which marriages are likely to endure happily and which are more apt to run aground.

Being able to predict what emotions and reactions tend to lead a couple into troubled waters is crucial to improving a marriage's chances. Remember the heart-disease analogy: determining which risk factors lead to a heart attack is the first step toward preventing one. If you know that a patient has chest pains, a high cholesterol level, or atherosclerosis, you can bet that he or she is on a direct collision course with severe illness if changes aren't made. Similarly, it is possible to chart an unhappy marriage's tragic journey and carefully dissect where the couple went wrong and why. By pinpointing how marriages destabilize I believe couples will be able to find their way back to the happiness they felt when their marital adventure began.

The first cascade a couple hits as they tumble down the marital rapids is comprised of "The Four Horsemen of the Apocalypse," my name for four disastrous ways of interacting that sabotage your attempts to communicate with your partner. In order of least to most dangerous, they are *criticism, contempt, defensiveness,* and *stonewalling.* As these behaviors become more and more entrenched, husband and wife focus increasingly on the escalating sense of negativity and tension in their marriage. Eventually they may become deaf to each other's efforts at peacemaking. As each horseman arrives, he paves the way for the next. Here is how the horsemen can slowly, insidiously override a marriage that started out full of promise.

THE FIRST HORSEMAN: CRITICISM

When Eric and Pamela married fresh out of college, they were excited about planning their future together. They knew there would be lean years of scrimping and saving before they could afford a house, so they promised each other to be quite thrifty at first. But it soon became clear that they had differing notions of what frugality meant. Eric felt he was living up to their agreement by consenting to rent a smaller apartment than he would have liked and putting off major purchases like a new car. To Pamela, saving also meant clipping coupons and buying even inexpensive items only on sale. One afternoon, Eric came home from the supermarket with boneless chicken breasts and Pamela complained: "You spent a lot of money at the supermarket! Don't you know that boneless breasts cost twice as much as regular ones? I feel so frustrated when we spend more money than we should." Eric told her he was sorry she was so upset but thought she was making too big a deal out of a relatively small amount of cash, considering their overall budget. Pamela continued to insist that Eric had wasted money. The argument came to an abrupt end when he walked out of the kitchen in a huff.

Over the next year, the couple spent many happy times together but occasionally squabbled. Almost always, the topic was money. Pamela found herself complaining again and again about Eric's spending habits: he didn't always turn off the lights when he left a room; he once phoned his brother before the long-distance rates went down after 11 P.M.; he bought a new pair of leather gloves even though his old ones were still in pretty good shape. Eric didn't consider his wife's complaints justified—after all, these were petty amounts of money. They were already saving far more than they had hoped to. Sure they had to be careful, but they were hardly broke.

As time passed and Pamela found that her comments did not lead Eric to change his spending habits, something potentially damaging to their marriage occurred: rather than complain about his *actions*, she began to criticize *him*. To Pamela, Eric's spending habits became more than a mere difference of opinion. Now, when she discovered he'd bought a new set of barbells, she said, "Why did you buy those weights when you know I've been denying myself a new scarf all winter? You always do things like that—just think about yourself, of *your* needs. I always have to deny myself things because you spend so much! You just don't care."

The first horseman of the apocalypse—criticism—had just entered their bedroom.

On the surface, there may not seem to be much difference between complaining and criticizing. But criticism involves *attacking someone's personality or character—rather than a specific behavior— usually with blame*. When Pamela said, "You always do things like that—just think about yourself, of your needs," she assaulted *Eric*, not just his actions, and blamed him for being selfish and ignoring her sacrifice. For his part, Eric began to criticize Pamela as well. Why was she so negative? Why did she have to spend so much time chastising him over minor purchases instead of praising his all-around thriftiness. He told her she was the type of person who never had anything nice to say, who just wanted to give him a hard time.

Since few couples can completely avoid criticizing each other now and then, the first horseman often takes up long-term residence even in relatively healthy marriages. One reason is that criticizing someone is just a short hop beyond complaining, which is actually one of the *healthiest* activities that can occur in a marriage. Expressing anger and disagreement—airing a complaint—though rarely pleasant, makes the marriage stronger in the long run than suppressing the complaint.

The trouble begins if you feel that your complaints go unheeded (or if you never clearly express them) and your spouse just repeats the offending habits. Over time, it becomes more and more likely that your complaints will pick up steam. With each successive complaint you're likely to throw in your inventory of prior, unresolved grievances. Eventually you begin blaming your partner and being critical of his or her personality rather than of a specific deed. Or, if you have been stifling your complaints, they may one day explode in a barrage of criticism.

You may find it difficult at first to differentiate between complaint and criticism. As a general rule, a criticism entails blaming, making a personal attack or an accusation, while a complaint is a negative comment about something you wish were otherwise. To oversimplify, complaints could easily begin with the word *I*, and criticisms with the word *you*. For example, "I wanted the laundry to be finished by now so I could get to the mall before it closes," is a complaint. "You should have finished the laundry by now. You know I want to get to the mall today," is a criticism. The difference may seem like splitting hairs, but it really does feel far worse to be on the receiving end of a criticism rather than a complaint. A criticism is also more likely than a complaint to make your partner defensive.

In a criticism, the attack on your spouse's character can be expressed in a number of different ways: "You don't care." "You always put yourself first." "You're the type of person who always finds fault." One common form of criticism is to explicitly pass judgment on your mate: "You should know better than to leave the porch light on all night." "You shouldn't *ever* put coffee grinds in the garbage disposal." "You should be ashamed of the things you said to him." The word *should* sends a powerful message: you can almost see the wagging finger in front of your partner's face.

One common type of criticism is to bring up a long list of complaints. I call this "kitchen sinking" because you throw in every conceivable negative thing you can think of. For example: "I don't feel listened to by you, and you don't touch me very often. I asked you to do certain chores but you didn't. I'm just not having any fun." Such a long list of complaints has the same effect as a criticism of your partner's personality because it seems so pervasive and overwhelming.

Another form of criticism is to accuse your partner of betraying you, of being untrustworthy. "I *trusted* you to balance the checkbook and you let me down. How could you do this to me? Your constant recklessness amazes me!" In contrast, complaints don't necessarily finger the spouse as a culprit; they are more a direct expression of one's own dissatisfaction with a particular situation.

One wife I studied, Alice, found it just about impossible to avoid accusing her husband of betrayal when she tried to speak with him about marital issues. She had particular trouble discussing her unhappiness with their sex life because she feared that whenever she'd bring up the subject he would become verbally abusive. In truth, he did usually respond that way. But part of the reason he became angry was that she would quickly slide from complaining to accusing him of being untrustworthy, a particularly nasty form of criticism:

> ALICE: Well, just a couple of months ago, I told you about how I felt [regarding sex] and you just act like you forgot it all. I've probably told you similar things like that before and all you do is forget them. Of course, that was when you were drinking. You forgot everything then.

Alice is really saying that she feels betrayed: she entrusted her spouse with her worries about sex and he ignored them. So now, rather than complain about specific sexual concerns she has, she criticizes him by accusing him of betraying her (and, for good measure, snipes at him for his previous drinking). By doing this she has escalated the problem from a concern about their sex life to a flaw in his character, his untrustworthiness.

Unlike complaints, criticisms also tend to be generalizations. A telltale sign that you've slipped from complaining to criticizing is if global phrases like "you never" or "you always" start punctuating your exchanges.

———————— ● ————————

CRITICISM vs. COMPLAINT

What is the difference between complaint and criticism?
Complaint is a specific statement of anger, displeasure, distress, or other negativity. For example, "I am very upset that you didn't

ask me about how my day went but just talked about your day through all of dinner."

Criticism is much less specific: it is more global; it may have blaming in it. For example, "You never show any interest in me or my work. You just don't care about me."

Here are some typical phrases that can further help you distinguish between complaints and criticisms. Remember that when you complain you are attacking a specific action (or lack of action). When you criticize, you are attacking the person:

> *Complaint:* We don't go out as much as I'd like to.
> *Criticism:* You never take me anywhere.

> *Complaint:* It upset me when I came home and there were dirty dishes in the sink. This morning we agreed that you would wash them.
> *Criticism:* You left dirty dishes all over the kitchen *again*. You promised me you wouldn't. I just can't trust you, can I?

> *Complaint:* I expected you to come home right after work. When you didn't, it made me feel like you care more about going out with your friends than spending time with me.
> *Criticism:* I hate that you're the type of person who never thinks to call and tell me you'll be late coming home. You always leave me hanging. You care more about your friends than you do about our marriage.

If these descriptions of criticism sound reminiscent of your own marital exchanges, you're hardly alone. The slow slide from complaint to criticism is very common. In fact, if you look back at some of the exchanges between happily married volatile couples in chapter 2, you'll find occasional examples of criticisms in their conversations. To some people, criticism comes so naturally that they skip complaining and go directly to these personal, global attacks. They are the bosses who say, "You don't focus enough on your work" rather than, "Your memo is not detailed enough," and the spouses who say, "You just aren't capable of keeping the bathroom clean, are you?" rather than, "Could you close the lid to the toothpaste, please."

Being critical is not evil; it can begin innocently enough and is often the expression of pent-up, unresolved anger. It may be one of those natural self-destruct mechanisms inherent in all personal relationships. Problems occur when criticism becomes so pervasive—or one partner is so sensitive to it—that it corrodes the marriage. When that happens it heralds the arrival of the other, more foreboding horsemen that can drag you toward marital difficulty.

To get a sense of whether you or your spouse is overly critical, try answering the following questions soon after an argument.

———— • ————

SELF-TEST: ARE YOU A CRITIC?

This test looks at how you talk about the things that bother you. If possible, take this test soon after a discussion or disagreement with your spouse so that your actions and feelings are fresh in your mind. Or, think back to the last argument you had. Try to recall it with as rich detail as possible. What started the argument? What did each of you say? How did you feel when it was over? Then answer the following questions as if you had just finished that discussion. Again, both you and your partner should take this test, or you should take it a second time as you imagine your partner would answer it.

In the discussion that just occurred:

1. I thought it was very important to determine who was at fault.
You: Yes   No   Your Partner: Yes   No

2. I saw it as my job to present all of my complaints.
You: Yes   No   Your Partner: Yes   No

3. I tried to see patterns and analyze my partner's personality as part of my complaint.
You: Yes   No   Your Partner: Yes   No

4. I didn't complain until I felt very hurt.
You: Yes   No   Your Partner: Yes   No

5. I tried to make a general point instead of being specific about one situation or action.
You: Yes   No   Your Partner: Yes   No

6. I analyzed my partner's personality in addition to discussing specific actions that bothered me.
You: Yes   No   Your Partner: Yes   No

7. I let things build up for a long time before I complained.
You: Yes   No   Your Partner: Yes   No

8. I didn't censor my complaints at all. I really let my partner have it full force.
You: Yes   No   Your Partner: Yes   No

9. When I complained my emotions were very intense and powerful.
You: Yes   No   Your Partner: Yes   No

10. I complained in part to get things off my chest.
You: Yes   No   Your Partner: Yes   No

11. I did not state my complaints in a neutral manner.
You: Yes   No   Your Partner: Yes   No

12. I didn't try to be very rational when I stated what I thought was wrong.
You: Yes   No   Your Partner: Yes   No

13. When I complained I felt explosive inside.
You: Yes   No   Your Partner: Yes   No

14. When I complained I brought up my partner's faults.
You: Yes   No   Your Partner: Yes   No

15. There's no stopping me once I get started.
You: Yes   No   Your Partner: Yes   No

16. I resented having to bring up these issues in the first place.
You: Yes   No   Your Partner: Yes   No

17. I regret my tactless choice of words when I complained.
You: Yes   No   Your Partner: Yes   No

18. Whenever I bring up a problem I know I'm basically right.
You: Yes   No   Your Partner: Yes   No

19. Whenever I bring up a problem it is my goal to get my partner to see how I'm right.
You: Yes   No   Your Partner: Yes   No

20. It was my goal to get my partner to accept some blame for the problem.
You: Yes   No   Your Partner: Yes   No

21. When I complained I used phrases like "You always" or "You never."
You: Yes   No   Your Partner: Yes   No

Scoring: If you checked "yes" on more than seven items you are probably a good candidate for being a critic. Remember, criticism by itself is not malevolent—it's easy to shift from complaining to criticizing. For specific advice on rephrasing criticisms as complaints, see chapter 7.

THE CRITIC

	YES	NO
YOU		
YOUR PARTNER		

THE SECOND HORSEMAN: CONTEMPT

By their first anniversary, Eric and Pamela still hadn't resolved their financial differences. Unfortunately, their fights were becoming more frequent and more personal. Pamela was feeling disgusted with Eric. In the heat of one particularly nasty argument, she found herself shrieking: "Why are you always so irresponsible? You never pay attention to how much you spend. You're so selfish!" Fed up and insulted, Eric retorted: "Oh shut up. You're just a stingy cheapskate who doesn't know how to live. I don't know how I ended up with you anyway." The second horseman—contempt—had entered the scene.

What separates *contempt* from criticism is the *intention to insult* and *psychologically abuse* your partner. With your words and body language, you're lobbing insults right into the heart of your partner's sense of self. Fueling these contemptuous actions are negative thoughts about the partner—he or she is stupid, disgusting, incompetent, a fool. In direct or subtle fashion, that message gets across along with the criticism. Pamela herself was amazed at how easily Eric could push her anger button during their battles, and afterward she often felt a mix of righteousness and shame over her disgust toward him.

At first, this couple's major conflict had been about spending habits. But as that issue went unresolved and escalated, their anger began to pervade other areas of their interaction. When this happened they often ceased being able to admire each other, or to remember why they had fallen in love in the first place. As a consequence, they rarely complimented each other anymore, or expressed mutual admiration or attraction. The major characteristic of their relationship became abusiveness. The contempt was bulldozing over the positive aspects of their union and destabilizing their marriage.

What Pamela and Eric experienced is hardly uncommon. When contempt begins to overwhelm your relationship you tend to forget entirely your partner's positive qualities, at least while you're feeling upset. You can't remember a single positive quality or act. This *immediate decay of admiration* is an important reason why contempt ought to be banned from marital interactions. For example:

ERIC: Oh, well then, what are you saying now about me Pam?

PAMELA: My usual complaint that you never listen to me. We have financial needs that we just can't put off any longer. We need a vacation. Badly. But you just conveniently manage never to hear that one, don't you.

ERIC: Maybe I would feel more like listening to you my dear if you would be a little more careful with our finances.

PAMELA: I am careful with our finances. If you'd provide a little more money for us, the kind of care you ask for wouldn't be so necessary.

ERIC: Well. I didn't know I married a princess.

PAMELA: Well. I didn't know I married a failure.

Recognizing when you or your spouse is expressing contempt is fairly easy. Among the most common signs are:

Insults and Name-calling. These barbs are hard to miss: bitch, bastard, jerk, wimp, fat, stupid, ugly. Some couples are cruder, others more creative. The result is the same. In a marriage, words such as these are such dangerous assault weapons that they ought to be outlawed.

Hostile Humor. Here the contempt is covered with the thin veil of comic relief. Edward Albee's masterful dark comedy about a tumultuous marriage, *Who's Afraid of Virginia Woolf*, is filled with such repartee. The drama takes place one evening at the home of George, a history professor, and his wife, Martha, the daughter of the college president. At one point, Martha humiliates George in front of guests by pointing out that he has not risen to be head of the history department despite his long tenure at the college, and her father's position. She gleefully tells the guests that he is "bogged down" in the history department and then proceeds to call him "Swampy." In revenge, he tells her: "In my mind, Martha, you are buried in cement, right up to your neck. No . . . right up to your nose. . . . That's much quieter."

Mockery. This is the art of the subtle put-down. The spouse's words or actions are made fun of and ridiculed, to show he or she is not respected or trusted. For example, after a husband tells his wife, "I really do care about you," she replies sarcastically, "Oh *sure*, you really do care about me."

Body Language. In its most subtle form, contempt is communicated with a few swift changes of the facial muscles. Signs of contempt or disgust include sneering, rolling your eyes, and curling your upper lip. At times in our research, facial expressions offered the clearest clue that something was amiss between a couple. For example, a wife may sit quietly and offer her husband an occasional "go on, I'm listening" while he airs his grievances. But at the same time, she is picking lint off her skirt and rolling her eyes. Her true feelings—contempt—are written in body language.

To see whether you or your spouse has shifted from criticism to contempt, take the following self-test soon after a disagreement. Again, if your spouse does not take the test, you can take it twice. It can be difficult to take such a hard look at yourself, but the long-term payoff is a better marital relationship:

SELF-TEST: NO RESPECT

For each statement, circle "yes" or "no" depending on whether you generally agree with it.

1. When we were discussing an issue in our marriage, I couldn't think of much of anything I admired in my partner.
You: Yes   No   Your Partner: Yes   No

2. When I got upset I could see glaring faults in my partner's personality.
You: Yes   No   Your Partner: Yes   No

3. I just don't respect some of the things my partner does.
You: Yes   No   Your Partner: Yes   No

4. I tried to point out ways in which my partner was inadequate in a particular situation.
You: Yes   No   YOUR PARTNER: Yes   No

5. I found it hard to have much pride in my partner's qualities.
You: Yes   No   YOUR PARTNER: Yes   No

6. During the discussion I found myself putting my partner down.
You: Yes   No   YOUR PARTNER: Yes   No

7. There's not a whole lot to look up to in the way my partner goes about things.
You: Yes   No   YOUR PARTNER: Yes   No

8. My spouse can be pretty arrogant at times.
You: Yes   No   YOUR PARTNER: Yes   No

9. When my partner got negative I found myself thinking of insulting things to say back.
You: Yes   No   YOUR PARTNER: Yes   No

10. My spouse can be pretty smug at times.
You: Yes   No   YOUR PARTNER: Yes   No

11. My spouse was too stubborn to compromise.
You: Yes   No   YOUR PARTNER: Yes   No

12. When my partner was upset with me I wanted to turn the tables and counterattack.
You: Yes   No   YOUR PARTNER: Yes   No

13. I can't help feeling that there's a lot of stupidity in my partner's behavior.
You: Yes   No   YOUR PARTNER: Yes   No

14. It's hard for me to see my partner's point of view when I don't agree.
You: Yes   No   YOUR PARTNER: Yes   No

15. I often have no respect for my partner when we are discussing an issue.
You: Yes   No   YOUR PARTNER: Yes   No

16. I just get fed up with all the negativity.
You: Yes   No   YOUR PARTNER: Yes   No

17. I felt disgusted by my partner's attitudes.
You: Yes   No   YOUR PARTNER: Yes   No

18. My spouse can be pretty stupid at times.
You: Yes   No   YOUR PARTNER: Yes   No

19. I disapprove of my partner's behavior.
YOU: Yes   No   YOUR PARTNER: Yes   No

20. My spouse can be pretty inept at times.
YOU: Yes   No   YOUR PARTNER: Yes   No

21. It was hard to respect my partner when he or she was being that incompetent.
YOU: Yes   No   YOUR PARTNER: Yes   No

22. When my partner is upset with me I think of all the ways I've been let down in this marriage.
YOU: Yes   No   YOUR PARTNER: Yes   No

23. My spouse can be very selfish.
YOU: Yes   No   YOUR PARTNER: Yes   No

24. I often feel a sense of righteous indignation when my partner is expressing something negative.
YOU: Yes   No   YOUR PARTNER: Yes   No

25. When I get dumped on I think of ways to get even.
YOU: Yes   No   YOUR PARTNER: Yes   No

26. When I see a glaring fault in my partner I can't recall my partner's positive qualities.
YOU: Yes   No   YOUR PARTNER: Yes   No

Scoring: If you answered "yes" to more than seven items you are probably a good candidate for using contempt.

CONTEMPT

	YES	NO
YOU		
YOUR PARTNER		

Remember that it is easy to feel overly critical at times, even in the best relationships, and it is human to state criticism in a contemptuous way now and then. If your score suggests that contempt is a problem for you, be sure to read about internal scripts in the next chapter. This will help you understand why you often respond to your spouse with contempt, and set you on the road to changing.

In brief, the best way to neutralize your contempt is to stop seeing arguments with your spouse as a way to retaliate or exhibit your superior moral stance. Rather, your relationship will improve if you approach your spouse with precise complaints (rather than attacking your partner's character) and express a healthy dose of admiration—the opposite of contempt—for your spouse. For specifics on putting this advice to work in your relationship, see chapter 7.

THE THIRD HORSEMAN: DEFENSIVENESS

Once contempt entered their home, Eric and Pamela's marriage went from bad to worse. A major reason: the third horseman—defensiveness—followed close behind. When either of them acted contemptuously, the other responded defensively, which just made matters worse. Now they both felt victimized by the other—and neither was willing to take responsibility for setting things right. In effect, they both constantly pleaded innocent:

> PAMELA: So, once again you didn't pay the credit card on time and now we have to pay a penalty. I don't know how I ended up with such an irresponsible man.
>
> ERIC: It was your turn to pay the bills this month, not mine.
>
> PAMELA: Now you're going to lie to get out of this?
>
> ERIC: You're the liar! Last month we agreed that you would handle the bills this month.
>
> PAMELA: Only because you're too irresponsible to be trusted with them. But I wasn't supposed to start paying till *next* month.
>
> ERIC: That's not true.
>
> PAMELA: You are so full of it!

What's happened between Pamela and Eric in this discussion is a classic case of contempt leading to defensiveness. It's easy to see why this happens. If you are being bombarded with insults, the natural inclination is to defend yourself from attack: "Leave me alone. What are you picking on me for? I didn't do anything wrong. It's not my fault." It has become a reflex, like blinking your eyes if a bug is buzzing near them or shooting your arms in front of you if you're about to be hit.

The fact that defensiveness is an understandable reaction to feeling besieged is one reason it is so destructive—the "victim" doesn't see anything wrong with being defensive. But defensive phrases, and the attitude they express, tend to escalate a conflict rather than resolve anything. If you are being defensive (even if you feel completely right-eous in your stance), you are adding to your marital troubles.

Sometimes people aren't aware of how defensive they are when their spouse attempts to communicate with them. Playing the innocent victim can take many forms, some more subtle than others. Although defensiveness is especially common in response to contempt, there are people who also react this way to criticism or even neutral complaints. If you or your spouse frequently exhibit any of the following defensive behaviors, the third horseman has settled into your relationship. Re-member that however it is expressed, defensiveness is fundamentally an attempt to protect yourself and ward off a perceived attack. It doesn't mean that you and your spouse are bad people or intentionally sab-otaging your relationship. By becoming familiar with these signs of defensiveness in its various forms, you'll be better able to recognize them for what they are when they occur in your discussions:

Denying Responsibility. No matter what your partner charges, you insist in no uncertain terms that you are not to blame. If your partner complains that the house is always dirty, you respond that it's not your fault because you can't do everything. If your husband yells at you for not laundering his clothes, you shoot back that you never said you were going to. If your wife says you hurt her feelings with some comments you made at the party, you reply that you didn't say anything wrong.

Making Excuses. In this defensive maneuver you claim that ex-ternal circumstances beyond your control forced you to act in a certain way. Your husband attacks you for being irresponsible and always late. Your response: "I couldn't get home on time because the freeway was jammed." (But why didn't you take an alternate route or leave extra time for the trip?). Your wife calls you a liar because you didn't tell her that you got a bonus at work. Your response: "If I told you, you'd just spend it all."

Disagreeing with Negative Mind Reading. Sometimes, your spouse will make assumptions about your private feelings, behavior, or motives. When this "mind reading" is delivered in a negative manner, it may trigger defensiveness in you. In the exchange below, Bruce keeps second-guessing his wife's negative feelings about the amount of time he spends on his hobby, writing science fiction stories. She becomes increasingly defensive as he distorts her point of view.

BRUCE: Well, what do you think about that? You hate it. I know you hate it! [Negative mind reading.]

NAOMI: It's not that I hate it. It's just that I hate to see your art go to waste.

BRUCE: But you think it's going to waste now in science fiction. [Negative mind reading.]

NAOMI: No I don't. I know that's what you like to do.

BRUCE: But don't you think that's going to be a waste?

NAOMI: No.

Cross-Complaining. This is a grown-up version of "so's your old man." You meet your partner's complaint (or criticism) with an immediate complaint of your own, totally ignoring what your partner has said. For example:

SUE: We don't ever have people over for dinner anymore. You're so antisocial.

BOB: No, it's just that you never clean up the place so we could.

JASON: I don't like it that your sister comes over every Saturday.

AMANDA: Well, I don't like it that you go to the gym every other night.

Lauren and Steve fell into the cross-complaining trap when discussing his recent purchase of a gun without telling her. He knew guns upset her. To make matters worse, he kept the gun—and payments he made on it—a secret for several months:

> LAUREN: That really makes me mad, that you can keep a secret from me for that long. I thought we didn't have secrets.
>
> STEVE: Well, remember when you got the car seat? You hid that from me, thinking I'd be unhappy until it was already paid off.

Rubber Man/Rubber Woman. Remember that old playground saw, "I'm rubber, you're glue. Whatever you say bounces off me and sticks to you"? In one move you manage to not only defend yourself from attack but blame your partner. So if your partner says he/she found your behavior at the party rude, you immediately counter with "*I'm* rude? You're the one who can't even remember to send my mother a birthday card."

In its most blatant form, this defense sounds like:

> BOB: Lazy! You never help with the dishes.
>
> SUE: That's not true, you're the one who never helps.

Sometimes the message is more subtle. For example, Rubber Man Carl and his wife Sara are discussing his drinking problem.

> SARA: When you drink too much you're just not sociable anymore, I feel separate from you. That's the part I fear.
>
> CARL: How about when you explode into a tantrum? Is that any different?
>
> SARA: Why are you asking me?
>
> CARL: Because I want to know how you feel when it's in your court and not mine.

Carl is defending himself from attack by turning the tables on his wife—*she's* the one who's not sociable.

Yes-Butting. A yes-but is any statement that starts off agreeing but ends up disagreeing. For example, suppose you think you did something you shouldn't have, but you have a morally justifiable reason that far outweighs the transgression.

SAM: You said you were going to fill up the gas tank and you didn't!

ELLEN: Yes, but that's because I had to get home in time to make dinner for your parents.

MELINDA: Once again, you let me down. You were supposed to pay the phone bill last week!

ANTHONY: Yes, but I was waiting for you to tell me you'd made a bank deposit first.

Repeating Yourself. Rather than attempting to understand the spouse's point of view, couples who specialize in this technique simply repeat back their own position to each other again and again. Both think they are right and that trying to understand the other's perspective is a waste of time. Here, Jonathan and Maria attempt to discuss whether he plays golf too often. Essentially, she keeps saying he does, he keeps saying he doesn't. They get nowhere.

MARIA: I think playing one day on the weekend is fine. But three or four nights a week is too much.

JONATHAN: Well, that's not much. It's a minimum.

MARIA: Not when you have two boys that need you home for dinner.

JONATHAN: I'd like to be home for dinner always, but if you play golf you have to play regularly.

MARIA: Well you don't have to play three or four times and then on the weekend. That's too much when you have a young family.

JONATHAN: I have to play often; otherwise it's not worth playing at all and I don't want to give up golf.

Both of them keep rephrasing and restating his or her point of view *without* paying an iota of attention to what the other is saying. They are hoping that if they express their opinion often enough—and loudly enough—eventually their partner will see the wisdom of their position and acquiesce.

Whining. This refers less to what you say than *how* you say it—childishly, with a high-pitched nasal tone and stressing one syllable toward the end of the sentence. "You never take me *any*where." "I told you to see a *doc*tor." "Why don't you *lis*ten to me?" The message is, "It's not fair. Why are you picking on me? I didn't do anything wrong. I'm totally innocent."

Karen fit this pattern when talking with her husband Bill about the money Karen's mother sent them each month. It was a small amount, but Bill resented it, in large part because his parents didn't help them out at all.

> BILL: What I'm saying is that I don't want the money. All right? And when you call her up, just don't talk about bills and what not.
>
> KAREN: I *don't*, all the time. I *don't*.

Body Language. Among the physical signs of defensiveness are a false smile (the corners of the mouth rise, but the eyes don't change), shifting the body from side to side (as if avoiding a punch), and folding your arms across your chest. Sometimes women who are feeling defensive play with their neck as if they were wearing a necklace.

———————— • ————————

THE KINDS OF DEFENSIVENESS

The essence of defensiveness is self-protection, a natural response to warding off a perceived attack.

CATEGORY	EXAMPLE
Denying responsibility	"It wasn't my fault." "It was your fault."
Making excuses	"The dog ate my errand list." "I couldn't help being late. If you'd have gotten the car fixed the way you said you would, I wouldn't have been late."

Disagreeing with negative mind reading	YOUR PARTNER: "You always get tense around my mom." YOUR DEFENSIVE RESPONSES: "I do not." "If you'd stand up for me when she criticizes me I wouldn't get so tense."
Cross-complaining	YOUR PARTNER'S COMPLAINT: "We never go out anymore!" YOUR CROSS-COMPLAINT: "You never want to make love!"
Rubber man/ rubber woman	YOUR PARTNER: "You don't listen to me." YOU: "Well you don't listen to me."
Yes-butting	"Yeah we could try that but it would be very impractical."
Repeating-yourself syndrome	"What I have been saying Pamela is that I think we ought to save more money and go on fewer trips."
Whining	We are all familiar with the whining sound, but it is also possible to whine without that sound, by feeling sorry for yourself and acting like an innocent victim. Whining conveys the message: "What are you picking on me for?"
Body language	Arms akimbo or folded across chest. Hands touch neck.

Of course, the major problem with defensiveness is that it obstructs communication. Rather than understanding each other's perspective you spend your discussions defending yourselves. Nothing gets resolved, so the conflict continues to escalate and more discussions characterized by attack and defensiveness occur.

To see whether you or your spouse is overly defensive, take the following self-test, preferably soon after a disagreement.

———— ● ————

SELF-TEST: HOW DEFENSIVE ARE YOU?

This quiz looks at whether you respond defensively when your partner brings up an issue. Try to recall your actual behavior, feelings, and thoughts just after an argument. It's very important that you be honest with yourself. For each statement, circle "yes" or "no" depending on whether you generally agree with it. Once more, if your partner does not take the test, you should take it twice.

1. When my partner complained, I felt unfairly picked on.
You: Yes   No   YOUR PARTNER: Yes   No

2. I felt misunderstood.
You: Yes   No   YOUR PARTNER: Yes   No

3. I don't feel that I get credit for all the positive things I do.
You: Yes   No   YOUR PARTNER: Yes   No

4. What went wrong was actually not that much my responsibility.
You: Yes   No   YOUR PARTNER: Yes   No

5. To avoid blame, I had to explain why and how the problem arose.
You: Yes   No   YOUR PARTNER: Yes   No

6. I felt unfairly attacked when my partner was being negative.
You: Yes   No   YOUR PARTNER: Yes   No

7. When my partner complained, I realized that I also had a set of complaints that needed to be heard.
You: Yes   No   YOUR PARTNER: Yes   No

8. My partner's negativity got too intense, too much, too out of proportion.
You: Yes   No   YOUR PARTNER: Yes   No

9. My partner was too touchy, got feelings hurt too easily.
You: Yes   No   YOUR PARTNER: Yes   No

10. There was some truth to my partner's complaints, but it was not the whole truth.
You: Yes   No   YOUR PARTNER: Yes   No

11. When my partner complained, I thought, "I am innocent of these charges."
You: Yes   No   YOUR PARTNER: Yes   No

12. When my partner complained I felt that I had to "ward off" these attacks.
You: Yes   No   YOUR PARTNER: Yes   No

13. I felt obligated to deny the complaints against me that were inaccurate.
You: Yes   No   YOUR PARTNER: Yes   No

14. When I listened to my partner's complaints I thought of complaints of my own that weren't getting attention.
You: Yes   No   Your Partner: Yes   No

15. My partner's views of the problem were too self-centered.
You: Yes   No   Your Partner: Yes   No

16. I thought, "What you say only bounces right off me."
You: Yes   No   Your Partner: Yes   No

17. When my partner complained I tried to think of ways to protect myself.
You: Yes   No   Your Partner: Yes   No

18. When my partner complained I thought of a way to reexplain my position.
You: Yes   No   Your Partner: Yes   No

19. When my partner complained I thought that if my position were really understood we wouldn't have all these issues.
You: Yes   No   Your Partner: Yes   No

20. It seems that all my partner can do is find fault with me.
You: Yes   No   Your Partner: Yes   No

21. Sometimes it feels like my partner is coming at me with a baseball bat.
You: Yes   No   Your Partner: Yes   No

22. During a hot argument I keep thinking of ways to retaliate.
You: Yes   No   Your Partner: Yes   No

Scoring: If you've checked "yes" for seven or more items, then you are probably a good candidate for being defensive. It is easy to feel unfairly attacked at times, even in the best relationship. People who score high in defensiveness often operate with an internal script of thoughts that maintain their distress. This is explained in more detail in the next chapter. In general, the defensive person feels like an innocent victim: wronged, misunderstood, unfairly treated, and not appreciated.

DEFENSIVENESS

	YES	NO
You		
Your Partner		

The first step toward breaking out of defensiveness is to no longer see your partner's words as an attack but as information that is being strongly expressed. Try to understand and empathize with your partner. This is admittedly hard to do when you feel under siege, but it is possible and its effects are miraculous.

Research shows that if you are genuinely open and receptive when your partner is expecting a defensive response, your partner is less likely to criticize you or react contemptuously when disagreements arise.

Of course, this change won't occur over night. A partner who is used to getting a defensive response may be quite surprised and distrustful at first. He or she may actually escalate complaining as a way to test you. But if you are consistently nondefensive, your spouse will finally get the happy message. For more details on how to overcome defensiveness, see chapter 7.

THE FOURTH HORSEMAN: STONEWALLING

Eric and Pamela were nearing rock bottom. Exhausted and overwhelmed by Pamela's attacks, Eric eventually stopped responding, even defensively, to her accusations. Their marriage went from being marred by poor communication to being virtually destroyed by none. Once Eric stopped listening to Pamela, their relationship became extraordinarily difficult to repair. Instead of arguing about specific issues, every confrontation degenerated into Pamela screaming at Eric that he was shutting her out. "You never say anything. You just sit there. It's like talking to a brick wall." Sometimes Eric didn't react at all. On other occasions he would just shrug or shake his head, saying: "I can't ever get anywhere with you. You're always right." This pronouncement was usually followed by his leaving the room. Eric's withdrawal augured the arrival of the fourth horseman—stonewalling.

One evening Eric came home from work very tired. He had been thinking a lot about Pamela and he decided to buy her some flowers. But then, after working a bit too late, he rushed home, got caught in traffic, and was very late for dinner. He was worried that Pamela would be angry because one of her big complaints was that she wanted them to eat dinner on time. He hoped he could avoid a blowup.

Unfortunately, Pamela had had a very hard day. She had agreed to take care of her sister's six-year-old child, Naomi, who had turned out to be a holy terror that day. Not only did Naomi defy every one of Pamela's requests—even trying to run away in a shopping mall— but Naomi later had an asthma attack and Pamela had to rush her to the emergency room. There had been no time to make dinner and now Eric was late, and yet again he hadn't bothered to call and say he would be late. All of Pamela's frustrations from the day poured out on Eric as he walked in the door.

PAMELA: Again you are very late!

ERIC: Got caught in traffic. Sorry. What's for dinner?

PAMELA: I have had it up to my eyeballs today with stress and disappointments. This has been a terrible day. Don't you think you could have the consideration to call me if you know you're going to be late? We've been over this a hundred times.

ERIC: There was no chance to call you. [Eric picks up the paper and starts to read it.]

PAMELA: You worked late, didn't you? It wasn't all traffic that made you late.

ERIC: (*After a long pause in which Eric is trying to control his temper*) Yes I worked late, and yes, I am inconsiderate; but I'm also hungry and tired. What's for dinner?

PAMELA: I've got news for you. We're going out, Mister. I've made reservations at Arnie's at eight. [Pamela grabs Eric's newspaper and crumples it up.]

ERIC: I've got news for you. I'm not going to take this crap. I need a drink. See ya. [Eric storms out of the house, on his way to a local tavern.]

Stonewalling often happens while a couple is talking. The stonewaller just removes himself by turning into a stone wall. Usually someone who is listening reacts to what the speaker is saying, looks at the speaker, and says things like "Uh huh" or "Hmmm" to let the speaker know that he is tracking. But the stonewaller abandons these messages, replacing them with stony silence.

When we've interviewed stonewallers they often claim that they are trying to be "neutral" and not make things worse. They do not seem to realize that stonewalling itself is a very powerful act: it conveys disapproval, icy distance, and smugness. It is very upsetting to speak to a stonewalling listener. This is especially true when a man stonewalls a woman, and much less true when a woman stonewalls a man. Most men don't seem to get physiologically aroused when their wives stonewall them, but wives' heart rates go up dramatically when their husbands stonewall them. Furthermore, most stonewallers (about 85 percent of them) are men! So this is mainly a problem women have with their men.

Some stonewallers don't react at all when their spouse is upset with them. Others may offer monosyllabic mutterings or quickly change the subject. In some cases, like Eric's, stonewallers may actually remove themselves physically from confrontation. But whatever a particular stonewaller's style, the message to the spouse is the same: I am withdrawing, disengaging from any meaningful interaction with you. If either spouse refuses to communicate whenever conflict arises, it can be hard to heal a marriage.

The fourth horseman need not mark the end of a relationship. But if your interactions have deteriorated to this extent you are at great risk of caterwauling even farther down the marital cascade—becoming so overwhelmed by the negativity in your relationship that you end up divorced, separated, or living lonely, parallel lives in the same home. Once the fourth horseman becomes a regular resident, it takes a good deal of hard work and soul searching to save the marriage.

Our research has shown that men are more likely to become stonewallers than are women. The reason, I believe, may be biological. Men tend to be more physiologically overwhelmed than women by marital tension—for example, during confrontations a man's pulse rate is more likely to rise, along with his blood pressure. Therefore, men may feel a greater, perhaps instinctive, need to flee from intense conflict with their spouse in order to protect their health. (For more on how differences in gender influence marital difficulties, see chapter 5.) But once *either* spouse develops into a habitual stonewaller, the marriage becomes fragile.

Keep in mind that anyone may stonewall occasionally during an intense marital exchange. The key word here is *habitual*. To see whether you or your spouse has too much of a tendency to stonewall, you should both take the following self-test shortly after a disagreement.

SELF-TEST: STONEWALLING

This short quiz will help you determine whether you are apt to stonewall during marital conflict. For each statement, circle "yes" or "no" depending on whether you generally agree or disagree with it. Take the test twice, if your partner does not take it.

1. When my partner complained I felt that I just wanted to get away from this garbage.
You: Yes   No   YOUR PARTNER: Yes   No

2. I had to control myself to keep from saying what I really felt.
You: Yes   No   YOUR PARTNER: Yes   No

3. I thought, "It's best to withdraw to avoid a big fight."
You: Yes   No   YOUR PARTNER: Yes   No

4. I withdrew to try to calm down.
You: Yes   No   YOUR PARTNER: Yes   No

5. When we have a big blowup, I just want to leave.
You: Yes   No   YOUR PARTNER: Yes   No

6. At times when my spouse is very negative, I think it is best just not to respond at all.
You: Yes   No   YOUR PARTNER: Yes   No

7. I'd rather withdraw than get my feelings hurt.
You: Yes   No   YOUR PARTNER: Yes   No

8. I think that sometimes withdrawing is the best solution.
You: Yes   No   YOUR PARTNER: Yes   No

9. I wondered why small issues suddenly became big ones.
You: Yes   No   YOUR PARTNER: Yes   No

10. I withdrew when my partner's emotions seemed out of control.
You: Yes   No   YOUR PARTNER: Yes   No

11. I thought, "I don't have to take this kind of treatment."
You: Yes   No   YOUR PARTNER: Yes   No

12. I didn't want to fan the flames of conflict, so I just sat back and waited.
You: Yes   No   YOUR PARTNER: Yes   No

13. I hate it when things in our discussions stop being rational.
YOU: Yes   No   YOUR PARTNER: Yes   No

Scoring: If you checked "yes" to four or more items you are probably a good candidate for being a stonewaller.

STONEWALLING

YES   NO

YOU
YOUR PARTNER

It is easy to feel overwhelmed and to want to run away from conflict at times, or to feel like not responding out of fear of increasing the tension. Often, a stonewaller thinks that he is simply being neutral rather than being disapproving or removed. It is important to realize that withdrawal during an argument is a very powerful act. When you don't provide feedback (by verbally interacting or simply nodding your head) it is quite unnerving to the speaker. He or she often responds by becoming all the more upset. It's much better to hang in there, perhaps to say that you feel like running away rather than actually acting on the emotion. For specifics on combating stonewalling, see chapter 7.

THE CYCLE OF NEGATIVITY

What makes the four horsemen so deadly to a marriage is not so much their unpleasantness but the intensive way they interfere with a couple's communication. They create a continuing cycle of discord and negativity that's hard to break through if you don't understand what is happening. Eric and Pamela are a classic example. Their happy marriage first became blighted when they moved from complaining about specific actions to *criticizing* each other's intrinsic nature. From there it was a slow but easy slide to feeling and *expressing contempt* toward each other. Not surprisingly, this mutual psychological abuse made it all the harder for them to listen intently to each other's point of view. Instead, they responded to the vicious attacks by *defending* themselves. They each perceived themselves as an innocent victim and their spouse as an evil, abusive figure. Who wants to understand someone else's perspective when you feel under siege? Finally, Eric became so overwhelmed by the stress and tension that he ceased interacting with his wife at all. He began *stonewalling*. Once Eric and Pamela moved from poor communication to virtually no communication, they were sliding closer toward the end of their marriage.

Eventually Eric and Pamela became so hurt and defensive that they heard only the negativity in what each other said. There were long cycles in which one negative response was met with another. There seemed to be no way out of their trap. What had happened to them?

In every marriage some interactions don't go very well. Fortunately, in most relationships there are ways of fixing things. I call these *repair mechanisms*, ways of trying to make things better. Often they are comments about the process of communication itself, like "Please let me finish," or "We're getting off the topic," or "That hurt my feelings."

These repair attempts often are needed most when people are frustrated and angry, and so they are often said with some irritation, or hurt, or even accompanied by an insult or a threat. But they are repair mechanisms nonetheless. In well-functioning marriages the negative parts of these messages are ignored, so the repair attempt works. But in marriages that are burdened by the cycle of negativity partners seem unable to ignore the negativity (perhaps that's all they hear). They respond with another negative statement and the repair attempt. In a satisfying marriage a statement like "We're off the topic" said with irritation is responded to with a stabilizing, "Sorry, let's get back to the budget." In an ailing marriage "We're off the topic" said with irritation is responded to with "I don't care if we're off the stupid topic! What I'm trying to say is . . ."

Fortunately, the story doesn't have to end with the four horsemen. There is still room to save a marriage, even at this point of great distress.

MARITAL MUDDLES AND WHEELS WITHIN WHEELS

On the surface it may seem like simple common sense that contempt or defensiveness can ruin communication between spouses. But through our research we have come to understand exactly how this transpires—and the answer is not all that obvious. When we compared fights between healthy couples in stable marriages with those that were in trouble, one difference stood out. The happily married used certain phrases and actions during an argument that prevented negativity from spiraling out of control. In effect, these conciliatory gestures, that is, repair mechanisms, act as a glue that helps to hold the marriage together during tense times. The four horsemen do harm by blocking a couple's ability to use these aids.

Different couples employ various types of repair mechanisms. As a general rule, though, they often entail commenting on what's happening in your interaction while it is taking place, or reminding your partner that you admire and empathize with him or her despite the conflict. Some typical repair mechanisms include saying, "Yes, I see." "Uh huh." "Go on"—all those little psychological strokes at which stable couples are masters. But volatile couples use them too, whereas avoidant couples don't need them as much because they don't let things get that tense very often.

Repair mechanisms also include phrases like "Stop interrupting me," or "That's off the subject. We were talking about how to keep the house clean, not whether we can afford a vacation," or "It really hurt my feelings when you said I looked heavier." The many different kinds of repair mechanisms that stable couples use during arguments are described in fuller detail in chapter 8. What is important to know now is that these mechanisms counteract defensiveness and deescalate tension. Without them, the marriage may become like a powerful heating system burdened with a broken thermostat. Lacking that inner check or regulation, it is in danger of exploding.

An important reason couples get off track is that they are unable to hear each other's attempts to mend the rift through the din of their anger and anxiety. Repair mechanisms are often not spoken in a tone that would impress Miss Manners. In fact, in the course of our research I was surprised to find how often even happily married couples can be downright rude to each other. Though marriage counselors may recommend refined discourse along the lines of "Please share your feelings with me, dear," real-life repair mechanisms are often accompanied by a growl, whine, or complaint. For example, rather than saying, "Please listen to me," a wife may demand, "Are you going to stop interrupting me already?" The husband yells in response, "Yeah, so, talk!" Fortunately, repair mechanisms needn't always be offered with great civility or even courtesy in order to be effective.

One reason some people have stable marriages may simply be that they are good at listening past the edge in their partner's voice to the positive or at least grudgingly conciliatory message behind it. They respond to the repair mechanism rather than the bitter coating. In unstable marriages a couple may be working very hard to figure out what is going wrong between them, but they get distracted by each other's negative messages. They may make attempts to repair the interactions but the negativity blocks the way. Like a car stuck in the mud, they frantically spin their wheels but get nowhere. What makes this especially tragic is that both partners probably can problem solve well when confronted with a difficulty not related to their marriage. In those circumstances they are able to use repair mechanisms easily. But as negativity comes to engulf their marriage, they lose access to these fundamental skills when dealing with each other.

One result of getting nowhere is that you may end up creating ever more elaborate and complex hypotheses for why your marriage isn't working. This occurs especially if you tend to be analytical by nature or psychologically sophisticated. What you get is what I call "wheels within wheels"—the problems in your relationship seem so overwhelmingly complex and incoherent that you despair of ever being able to navigate your way out of the mire. For a brief example, take David and Laura, married for four turbulent years. Over time, Laura settled on an explanation for why she and her husband fought so frequently. She concluded that he was trying to dominate her. She looked at his family and found quick confirmation of this theory. After all, his father dominated his mother. No wonder David wanted to control her. Soon she was throwing her theory out at him during their arguments:

DAVID: You shouldn't blame yourself every time Bobby misbehaves.

LAURA: Don't tell me how to feel. Stop trying to dominate me!

DAVID: Shut up! I'm not trying to dominate you.

LAURA: You see, there you go again! You're exactly like your Dad. Don't tell me to shut up!

Laura doesn't hear the repair mechanism coming through David's irritation and frustration—she doesn't hear him say explicitly that he is not trying to dominate her. All she hears is the negativity, the "shut up!" She uses what she hears to further confirm her analysis of what's wrong with him. Result: an impasse. Imagine how differently their argument would end if it began like this:

DAVID: You shouldn't blame yourself every time Bobby misbehaves.

LAURA: Don't tell me how to feel. Stop trying to dominate me!

DAVID: Shut up, I'm not trying to dominate you!

LAURA: You're not?

DAVID: No.

LAURA: Because when you tell me I shouldn't feel a certain way it sounds like you're trying to control my life.

DAVID: I'm not. I'm just trying to be helpful.

David might even end up apologizing for telling her to "shut up," explaining that it frustrates him enormously when she falsely accuses him.

It may be that some couples get caught in these wheels within wheels because they have unrealistic expectations of how a spouse is likely to behave in marriage. When their beloved turns nasty in the heat of battle, or after a hard day at work, they read more into it than is really there.

Clearly, "The Four Horsemen of the Apocalypse" are so dangerous to your marriage because they sabotage your attempts to keep negativity from overwhelming your relationship. By unsettling a marriage's healthy ecology—that 5-to-1 ratio in favor of positive interaction—

the horsemen can throw a happy couple into a disastrous tailspin.

But these four horsemen comprise only the first of two cascades toward marital dissolution, not the end of the line. It is only after they turn a relationship sour that the ultimate danger arises: partners seize on powerful thoughts and beliefs about their spouse that cement their negativity. Only if these inner thoughts go unchallenged are you likely to topple down the final marital cascade, one that leads to distance and isolation. However, if you learn to recognize what is happening to your once-happy marriage, you can still develop the tools you need to regain control of it.

FOUR

YOUR PRIVATE THOUGHTS
BECOME CAST IN STONE

In a memorable scene from Woody Allen's movie, *Annie Hall*, Annie and Alvie, who have just met over a doubles tennis match, have drinks on the roof of her apartment building. On the surface, their conversation is about critiquing the art of photography, but they are really deciding whether to become romantically involved. While they chatter away about aesthetic guidelines, a far more important conversation is going on inside each of their heads. Flashing subtitles show their private thoughts: "I wonder what she looks like naked," Alvie muses. "I hope he doesn't turn out to be a schmuck like the others," Annie tells herself. These inner thoughts hold the key to what happens between them. It shows their self-consciousness and uncertainty—and their mutual attraction. By the end of their conversation, it becomes clear that they will start dating.

It's hardly surprising that what you think about someone often determines how you'll treat them. But when it comes to marriage, this simple truth has huge consequences. The assumptions you make about your spouse and your relationship can determine the state of your marriage's health. Marital problems easily arise if your thoughts and feelings are distorted—if your "subtitles" reinforce a negative view of your partner and your marriage. The more entrenched the four horsemen become in your relationship, the more likely that your internal script will take on a decidedly negative tone. Once this occurs, you're at great risk for feeling so overwhelmed by the negativity that you enter the final leg of the marital rapids, what I call the "Distance and Isolation Cascade."

Because most of us trust our feelings and intuitions, it's not so easy to recognize when your inner script is distorted. Consider these two scenarios. In the first, Bill comes home grouchy and starts yelling that the house is a mess. His wife Betty thinks: "Boy, is he in a bad mood. This is really upsetting me. I hope he gets over it once he unwinds. I wonder what's going on at work that's making him so tense?"

In scenario 2, Bob comes home grouchy and starts yelling that the house is a mess. His wife Jane thinks: "I'm really upset by his yelling. He is always such a grouch. Besides, since when is housecleaning only *my* responsibility? He is such a sexist pig. I can't believe I have to put up with this!"

Although the husbands displayed exactly the same behavior in both scenarios, obviously there's quite a contrast in Betty and Jane's inner thoughts. Both women feel understandably stressed by their husband's outburst. But the key difference is how they channel their stressful feelings. During this upsetting episode, Betty's thoughts are *self-soothing*. She reminds herself that her husband Bill isn't always like this, that the problem is probably tension he is feeling at work. Jane's thoughts, on the contrary, are *distress maintaining*. Her negative thoughts about Bob probably make her even more upset than his anger warrants.

Since people usually end up acting in accordance with what they are thinking and feeling, Betty and Jane are likely to respond in dramatically different ways. Because Betty's thoughts have soothed rather than agitated her, she will probably approach Bill lovingly—trying to soothe him in turn. She may calmly let him know that she recognizes how upset he is about the house, perhaps even point out to him how unusually stressed he seems to be, even crack a joke. In the best possible outcome, her empathic approach will help him link his surface agitation about housecleaning to the real cause of his anger—his lousy day at work. But even if Bill doesn't make that connection, his wife's response will prevent his outburst from triggering a counterproductive fight.

Jane, however, is more likely to respond defensively, perhaps counterattacking or stonewalling. Rather than repair what's happening between her and Bob, either reaction will just escalate the conflict and further reinforce her negative view of him. This couple's tumble down the marital rapids will continue.

I wish I could say that it is common during times of marital conflict to have soothing thoughts like Betty's. But as you are probably well aware from personal experience, most of us are a lot more like Jane. We tend to have distressing thoughts when we're feeling angry, hurt, or misunderstood—especially if the four horsemen have infiltrated our marriage.

The couples I have studied were no exception. In one experiment, for example, we asked newlyweds to come back and watch videos of their conversations recalling for us what they were actually thinking during incidents in their marriage when they acted hostile, defensive, or withdrawn. The vast majority were having very distressing thoughts. When we looked closely at these thoughts we found that, amazingly, they fell into only two major categories: thoughts of *innocent victimhood* or thoughts of *righteous indignation*. Some people expressed both at the same time.

THE INNOCENT VICTIM

If you are hit hard by the third horseman, defensiveness, you are likely to have innocent-victim thoughts during fights with your spouse. The major emotion you probably feel then is fear, and you see your spouse as an attacking monster and yourself as put upon, unfairly accused, mistreated, unappreciated. If you look back at some of the signs of defensiveness described in chapter 3 (whining, yes-butting, rubber man/woman, repeating-yourself syndrome), it's not hard to see that thoughts of innocent victimhood can trigger these responses. A stonewaller, too, is likely to be feeling like an innocent victim—so fearful and overwhelmed that he or she can't even express defensiveness.

To give you more of an idea of what innocent-victim thoughts sound like, here are what some newlyweds in our study said they were thinking or feeling during particularly distressing moments with their spouses:

He was blaming me for overcommitting us to a lot of things we then have to go and do, like it's my fault that I plan for social events. I feel like I can't do anything right for him. I don't understand what he wants. I wish he would understand all the things I do for us and appreciate them, making schedules for us for social events. He acts like everything he does is right and I'm the only one who does anything wrong.

I wanted to leave the party, but she was having too good a time, so she just dismissed me and my feelings. She told me that I act this way typically at parties, that I'm antisocial, and she is tired of it and just wants to have a good time. I felt hurt and put down. There's a lot I do at parties to make sure we have a good time and none of this gets recognized.

We went to buy a sewing machine and it got down to two and he left me to decide which one to get and I picked the one that was more expensive. Then he made this face at the checkout register and I brought them both back. I felt accused and embarrassed. I accused him of wanting me to buy the cheaper one but setting it up so he pretended that the choice was mine. But it was not really mine.

When she starts a fight I just drop the subject and then I apologize. It's usually pretty painful. I think that I don't really trust her. If I say what's on my mind there will be a big confrontation and it is easier to just give in and then we can drop this topic. I have apologized about things I have no understanding of. If I keep talking about it, it will get more and more of a mess. I want to get away from this kind of conversation as soon as I can.

Thinking of yourself as an innocent victim has certain benefits (if it didn't, not so many people would do it!). By mentally freeing yourself of any responsibility for the conflict, you don't have to do any work to save your marriage. But that's exactly the problem with this way of thinking. Of course you feel completely justified in feeling victimized (no doubt, you think your spouse has been acting pretty nastily). But for as long as you excuse yourself from repairing the relationship, your marital problems are unlikely to improve.

RIGHTEOUS INDIGNATION

This inner script is similar to the innocent victim, but also includes hostility and contempt toward your spouse for trying to victimize you. People who are hit hard by contempt, the second horseman, often have inner scripts filled with righteous indignation. They are hurt and angry and want revenge. Again, stonewallers may also be harboring these thoughts, which fuels their fuming in silence. Here are some thoughts of righteous indignation expressed by women in our newlywed study.

> He was getting very defensive about my comments about his driving. He didn't take what I was saying seriously at all. He was going real fast; meanwhile I'm holding on for my life and yelling at him to slow down. So if I make a comment I'm being a bitch and he's a poor sad sack who is victimized by this evil bitch. Can't he just accept my feelings and slow down?

> I feel like he's manipulating me and I want to get out of it and strike back. I feel trapped and confused. But mostly I am thinking of getting even.

> He thinks I don't take his needs into account more, but why should I always have to?

> So what's he trying to do, catch me in a lie? He is jealous, but instead of this being his problem it is *my* problem and I have to make him feel more secure? Well, screw that. Maybe I should try a bit harder to see it from his perspective, but I don't want to. It's ridiculous.

Obviously, these kinds of thoughts are hardly conducive to healing a marital rift. It may take a lot of courage and self-awareness to prevent yourself from falling into the righteous indignation or innocent-victim trap. The first step toward changing your inner script is to identify which of the two types of distress-maintaining thoughts you tend to have. To find out, take the following self-test soon after a spat:

SELF-TEST: DISTRESS-MAINTAINING THOUGHTS

During our last discussion:
1. I felt hurt.
   Yes   No

2. I felt misunderstood.
   Yes   No

3. I thought, "I don't have to take this."
   Yes   No

4. I felt innocent of blame for this problem.
   Yes   No

5. I thought to myself, just get up and leave.
   Yes   No

6. I was scared.
   Yes   No

7. I was angry.
   Yes   No

8. I was worried.
   Yes   No

9. I felt disappointed.
   Yes   No

10. I wanted my feelings to get some attention here.
    Yes   No

11. I felt unjustly accused.
    Yes   No

12. I thought, "My partner has no right to say those things."
    Yes   No

13. I felt let down.
     Yes   No

14. I felt sad.
     Yes   No

15. I was frustrated.
     Yes   No

16. I felt personally attacked.
     Yes   No

17. I wanted to strike back.
     Yes   No

18. I felt like I was warding off a barrage.
     Yes   No

19. I felt like getting even.
     Yes   No

20. I wanted to protect myself.
     Yes   No

21. I knew I was right.
     Yes   No

22. I had a pretty low opinion of my partner's personality at the time.
     Yes   No

Scoring
1. Tally the number of "yes" responses to statements 1, 2, 4, 5, 6, 8, 11, 13, 14, 16, 18, and 20. A score of 4 or more suggests you tend to have an *innocent-victim* reaction during negative times in your marriage.
2. Tally your "yes" responses to statements 1, 2, 3, 7, 9, 10, 12, 15, 17, 19, 21, 22. A score of 4 or more suggests you tend to have a *righteous-indignation* reaction during negative times in your marriage.

If you scored high in either category (or both), you are rehearsing negative thoughts during conflict with your spouse. You can't change your mate's inner thoughts, but you can work on changing your own and on soothing both of you. This will make you feel less victimized and/or angry. Replacing your distorted negative script with a more realistic one won't happen overnight. But many couples have successfully done this and seen their marriage improve dramatically as a result. For specifics on how to soothe, see chapter 7.

FEELING FLOODED

The worst consequence of a negative inner script is that it can lead to *flooding*. When this occurs you feel so overwhelmed by your partner's negativity and your own reactions that you experience "systems overload," swamped by distress and upset. You may become extremely hostile, defensive, or withdrawn. Once you're feeling this out of control, constructive discussion is impossible.

In any intense exchange with a spouse, it's normal for some negative thoughts and feelings to arise. As long as they don't get too extreme, most people are able to handle them. We each have a sort of built-in meter that measures how much negativity accumulates during such interactions. When the level gets too high for you, the needle starts going haywire and flooding begins. Just how readily people become flooded is individual. A rare few of us have very high thresholds and can listen to their spouse express contempt for hours without feeling overwhelmed. This is especially common in volatile couples. Others feel flooded at the mere suggestion of a complaint, especially in avoidant couples. Flooding is also affected by how much stress you have outside the marriage—the more pressure you're under, the more easily flooded you will be.

Between those two extremes, the rate at which people become flooded seems to break down along gender lines. It may surprise you, but we find that men become flooded far more easily than women. This explains why men are more likely to be stonewallers. In essence, their withdrawal represents a last-ditch attempt to protect themselves from feeling overwhelmed. (For more on this difference between the sexes, see chapter 5.)

But women are hardly immune to flooding. For example, watch how Yvonne is eventually overcome during an exchange with her husband that we videotaped in our lab. The topic is the jealousy she feels toward her husband's ex-girlfriends. It is clear that this is not an easy topic for her. Although she shifts back and forth between positive and negative feelings, she does not start to feel flooded until her husband makes a disturbing confession. Then, system overload sets in.

NICHOLAS: Well, the issue is your jealousy.

YVONNE: (*Calm*) Which has gotten a lot better lately.

NICHOLAS: Yes it has. Since I made a commitment to my family it has gotten better. Now if you saw me during the day driving in my car with a woman you wouldn't get jealous probably.

YVONNE: (*Slightly alarmed*) Why? Is there a woman in your car?

NICHOLAS: No.

YVONNE: (*Relieved*) Good.

NICHOLAS: Actually, Sara and I are going to ride together to a workshop.

YVONNE: (*Neutral*) A workshop? What about?

NICHOLAS: Commercial real estate. It's business.

YVONNE: (*Quite calm*) Oh. No I wouldn't be jealous of that.

NICHOLAS: You know it does bother me though, just for a hypothetical, that say I wanted to see Jeannie again, just say for lunch, you know.

YVONNE: (*Slightly alarmed*) No, Jeannie is a different story. You were lovers.

NICHOLAS: But that was way before I met you. And you know that I have made a commitment to our family. It is just not an issue. It's like seeing an old chum.

YVONNE: (*More relaxed—she perceives this as a hypothetical discussion*) It doesn't matter. That's a very different kind of relationship. She simply has no place in our lives. It's not like a chum. She's a woman.

NICHOLAS: See that's where I think you're wrong. She's a person that I once liked a lot, and it's a shame to lose touch with her. As a friend. As an acquaintance.

YVONNE: (*Clearly alarmed*) Why should she come into our lives, into our home? Why should my children know her?

NICHOLAS: She's very interesting. You both went to the same college. You have a lot in common.

YVONNE: (*Fearful*) Wait a minute! Do you want to see her? Is that what you are saying?

NICHOLAS: Yes I would. Why not? I'd like to find out how she's doing, talk to her again. Yes.

YVONNE: (*Flooded*) Then I think we have a serious problem. We need counseling.

NICHOLAS: Well, maybe we do.

Yvonne falls silent. She is temporarily too upset to continue the discussion. Although Yvonne teeter-tottered between positive and negative feelings throughout the conversation, by the end the negativity became overwhelming and she was flooded. Her internal script supplied more anxious-making information than she could calmly respond to.

How does it feel to be flooded? When people start to be flooded, they feel unfairly attacked, misunderstood, wronged, or righteously indignant. If you are being flooded, you may feel that things have gotten too emotional, that you just want things to stop, you need to calm down, or you want to run away. Or you may want to strike back and get even. You may feel you can't get your thoughts organized, or that this outburst of your partner's has come out of the blue, for no apparent reason. Typical thoughts of people being flooded include, "Things were going along pretty well, when suddenly this mess happened," or "My partner is turning into a monster out to get me."

The body of someone who feels flooded is a confused jumble of signals. It may be hard to breathe. People who are flooded inadvertently hold their breath. Muscles tense up and stay tensed. The heart beats fast and it may seem to beat harder. The flooded person longs for some escape and relief.

You can see flooding in George as he and his wife Vera discuss an issue in their marriage:

VERA: Our problem is that now we only have one car, and you have to get up an hour earlier and drive me to work. And you hate getting up in the morning.

GEORGE: Yeah, I'm a night person. [George is aware of the problem.

His view is that he is a night person and Vera is a morning person, and it's no big deal.]

VERA: You're a lazy person.

GEORGE: Now I have never been lazy. [George feels like he just got slapped. He is anything but a lazy person in his view. George's feelings are hurt.]

VERA: George, you'd be late every day if I didn't get you up.

GEORGE: (*Pouting*) I don't like you waking me up.

VERA: You'd rather get up with an alarm clock . . .

GEORGE: I would prefer it . . .

VERA: To the sound of my voice, is that it?

GEORGE: It does sort of remind me of my mom's voice nagging me to get up . . .

VERA: And you hate the sound of my voice in the morning.

GEORGE: It's not that. It's just that, how can I explain your voice, you see, um . . . [Now George realizes he is in hot water. His wife's temper is acting up again. He starts looking for a way out of this. He thinks if he can just get her to see how grating her voice can be in the morning. Maybe he can end this conversation. It's not going the way he wanted.]

VERA: (*Rising up to the heights of indignation*) I get up, I straighten the house, I fix your lunch, and then you can't stand to hear my voice. How is that supposed to make me feel, George?

GEORGE: Uh, pretty bad, I guess. Don't take it that way Vera. Just try to relax. [Feeling like a butterfly impaled on a pin, he knows he's had it. His heart is beating fast. He wants to backtrack.]

VERA: Don't you start telling me what feelings to have, George. I'll be hurt if I want to be. You hurt me.

GEORGE: I know how you feel about getting to work on time. And I really want to try to get up. [George feels like he wants to run out of the house.]

To get a sense of whether you tend to feel flooded during times of marital conflict, take the following test:

SELF-TEST: FLOODING

1. At times, when my partner gets angry I feel confused.
   Yes   No

2. Our discussions get far too heated.
   Yes   No

3. I have a hard time calming down when we discuss disagreements.
   Yes   No

4. I'm worried that one of us is going to say something we will regret.
   Yes   No

5. My partner gets far more upset than is necessary.
   Yes   No

6. After a fight I want to keep away for a while.
   Yes   No

7. There's no need to raise one's voice the way my partner does in a discussion.
   Yes   No

8. It really is overwhelming when an argument gets going.
   Yes   No

9. I can't think straight when my partner gets so negative.
   Yes   No

10. I think, "Why can't we talk things out logically?"
    Yes   No

11. My partner's negative moods come out of nowhere.
    Yes   No

12. When my partner's temper gets going there is no stopping it.
    Yes   No

13. I feel cold and empty after one of our fights.
    Yes   No

14. When there is so much negativity I have difficulty focusing my thoughts.
    Yes   No

15. Small issues suddenly become big ones for no apparent reason.
    Yes   No

16. I can never seem to soothe myself after one of our fights.
    Yes   No

17. Sometimes I think that my partner's moods are just crazy.
    Yes   No

18. Things get out of hand quickly in our discussions.
    Yes   No

19. My partner's feelings are very easily hurt.
    Yes   No

20. When my partner gets negative, stopping it is like trying to stop an oncoming truck.
    Yes   No

21. All this negativity drags me down.
    Yes   No

22. I feel disorganized by all this negative emotion.
    Yes   No

23. I can never tell when a blowup is going to happen.
    Yes   No

24. When we have a fight, it takes a very long time before I feel at ease again.
    Yes   No

Scoring: If you answered "yes" to more than eight statements, this is a strong sign that you are prone to feeling flooded during conflict with your spouse. Because this state can be harmful to your marriage, it's important to let your spouse know how you are feeling. The antidote to flooding is to practice soothing yourself and your mate. This will help change how you perceive your partner's negative reactions. Instead of feeling overwhelmed by your spouse's angry tone or words, try to see them simply as an underliner—a way for your partner to emphasize something he or she is feeling—rather than as a personal attack. For specific advice on recognizing underliners and learning how to soothe, see chapter 6.

THE BODY SPEAKS

One of our most exciting discoveries is evidence of a dramatic link between how our minds and bodies respond to marital upsets. In most of our studies, along with analyzing what couples say and how they say it, we have also measured their heart rates and other barometers of stress, such as how much they sweat and their adrenaline levels.

This has given us compelling evidence of how and when flooding operates during marital conflict as well as its consequences for marriage.

So much has been written about stress that most of us are aware that it has a powerful physical component. Under duress we tend to release excess amounts of stress hormones such as adrenaline that lead the heart to beat faster, the sweat glands to work overtime, and respiration to speed up. These physical symptoms of stress create a feedback loop with the anxiety-provoking thoughts and emotions we are experiencing. For example, you feel pressured by a work deadline, your heart starts racing, which just heightens your anxiety, making you think even more about the deadline, which raises your pulse even higher.

This is exactly what seems to happen when you become flooded during a marital conflict. In a sense, your negative inner thoughts and your aroused nervous system goad each other on, making it all the more difficult to break out of the cycle of negativity. Once your physical arousal reaches a certain level it becomes virtually impossible to think calm, soothing thoughts or to appreciate your spouse's point of view.

To see how flooding can begin during a negative interaction and then feed that negativity further, consider what happened to Bradley and Eloise during the following discussion. Bradley and Eloise tease each other often. They enjoy this style of interaction, one that is fairly typical in a volatile marriage (but not necessarily restricted to this type of marriage). She has teased him about his not being able to parallel park, and he then retaliates by teasing her about not being a very good lover. She is hurt and he is trying to convince her that he didn't mean it.

While they talked, we measured their heart rates. Under normal circumstances, the average man's resting heart rate or pulse is about 72 beats per minute (BPM), while a woman's is higher, about 82 BPM. My data suggest that when the heart rate goes up to about 80 BPM for a man and 90 BPM for a woman, the flooding process begins. At this level, physiological arousal makes it hard to focus on what the other person is saying, which leads to increased defensiveness and hostility. For either sex, if the heart rate skyrockets to 100 BPM, adrenaline is secreted in such large doses that it triggers a "fight or flight" stress reaction, with intense fear or anxiety.

Watch Bradley's heart rate as you read the following transcript. Before the conversation began his heart rate was in the normal range. He and his wife Eloise are a volatile couple who tease each other often. But this time, the ribbing got out of control when she gave him a hard time about his inability to parallel park. He eventually retaliated by suggesting she wasn't a good lover. Now he's trying to take it all back:

BRADLEY: I'm sorry about this morning.

ELOISE: Well, I think we should talk about it. Ever since the other night, you've been making fun of what I said.

BRADLEY: It's awfully mean of me to do that, and I'm sorry. And I don't think I'll do that anymore. It was just that you made me feel awful that I couldn't parallel park. And I had to get back at you somehow. And saying that was just another step meaner than what you said.

ELOISE: But there must be some truth to what you said.

BRADLEY: No, no. There's not any truth to it at all.

ELOISE: But there is truth to the fact that you can't parallel park. You said that yourself. I was just trying to point out that if there's something you can't do, that if you take a little time to practice, or let someone instruct, you could do it better.

BRADLEY: Can you parallel park the truck?

ELOISE: Yes. Bradley, I do. In downtown St. Louis. Almost every day.

BRADLEY: (*Exhales*) Oh, I can never do that.

ELOISE: But you can. See, if you say "I can't do it," then that means "I won't try." And my point of telling you about that, was that you—if you say "I won't try," then you can't.

BRADLEY: Right. [HIS HEART RATE: 80 BPM; this is already aroused.]

ELOISE: But if you make an effort, then you can.

BRADLEY: Right.

ELOISE: But the point is, you then made a very negative comment about my sexual abilities.

BRADLEY: (*Laughs*) But I didn't mean it. That's what you gotta understand. [HIS HEART RATE: 96.3 BPM. His heart rate has rocketed upward 16 BPM within the time of a single heartbeat! This is extreme arousal, and it is around the level when large amounts of adrenaline start getting secreted.]

ELOISE: But how do I know that?

BRADLEY: I'm telling you, and we're supposed to be honest with each other, and I am being.

ELOISE: (*Sigh*) But you know, sex is probably one of the issues that we have recurring problems about. Obviously it's real sensitive, or your teasing wouldn't upset me.

BRADLEY: Well . . . I think some of it is probably because our upbringing was different. And we have different . . . you know, points of view on it. [HIS HEART RATE EXCEEDS 100 BPM.]

ELOISE: How so?

BRADLEY: Well, I was always taught that it was never to be discussed.

ELOISE: You think my family's more open about that?

BRADLEY: Uh-huh. [His heart rate has now gone down to 82.4, still high, but a bit more relaxed.]

What happened in this conversation? For Eloise, sex is such a hot topic that her husband's criticism made her very upset. His attempts to backtrack and deny the tease lead him to feel flooded. In this state, it will be difficult for him to have a productive discussion with his wife.

THE DANGER OF CHRONIC FLOODING

It's certainly not unusual to feel flooded in the heat of an argument or during an uncomfortable discussion. But if this happens often enough, a catastrophic shift occurs in how you think about your spouse and your marriage. You start to react to everything your partner says and does with dread—"What now?" You become hypervigilant, continually on guard against an attack, and are continually immersed in your own distress-maintaining thoughts. Your wife says, "We've got to talk," and you automatically think, "Another fight is starting," and your body floods with distress—when she only wanted to talk about having the babysitter come early.

In short, you start to react to your spouse like an animal conditioned to fear a shock whenever it sees the color red. Show the red and the animal panics; let your spouse speak in a certain tone of voice or have a particular facial expression, and you react as though you had already been attacked. By this point distorted and distressing thoughts become the rule, not the exception. In effect, your negative internal script and your aroused body conspire to throw your meter into the negative range for good. If the meter isn't repaired, you'll be launched on the final cascade toward marital breakdown.

Once flooding becomes rampant, you are likely to think the worst of your spouse most of the time. In our research we have come across a fundamental difference between how couples perceive their day-to-day interactions depending on whether or not they feel frequently flooded. In a stable marriage, where flooding is not a problem, the partners tend to view each other through "rose-colored" glasses. They assume that each other's positive, admirable characteristics are an intrinsic part of their personality rather than occasional flukes. In other words, if a husband surprises his wife with a bouquet of flowers, she will see this as further confirmation that he is loving and generous by nature. She considers these assets part of his overall character and sees evidence of them in many areas of her life with him. On the other hand, when her husband acts grouchy or does something selfish, she attributes his negative actions to some short-lived, isolated incident— just as Betty assumed that Bill's foul mood was caused by trouble on the job. Sure he's angry now, she thinks, but he's not an angry person. Even if she is upset by his bad mood she will tend to edit her reaction so as not to return the anger. Happily married spouses view their marriage itself in the same glowing light that they see each other in. The good things about their relationship are considered stable and far-reaching while the bad patches or areas of tension are considered to be fleeting and situational.

What a difference from a marriage in which at least one partner has become chronically flooded! Such couples seem blind to evidence of good things in the marriage and recognize only the bad. Negative expectations and assumptions about the spouse and the relationship become the norm. Any evidence of a positive nature is ignored or treated suspiciously. A husband thinks: "Oh, well, she's being nice because she's been successful at work this week. It won't last and it doesn't mean much." He assumes the good in his wife is fleeting and caused by external factors (a good week at work) rather than her personality.

Over time, such couples pay ever more attention to their spouse's actions that confirm their negative assumptions, rather than those that could refute them. For example, Joe had concluded that his wife was untrustworthy and selfish. So, although she cooked him dinner almost every night one week, he only noticed the one night she ate out with friends. In this state, thoughts of contempt inevitably overrun thoughts of admiration and fondness for your spouse. The crucial 5-to-1 ratio of positive to negative needed to keep a marriage stable is easily destroyed.

How do things get so bad? Remember that if your inner script is dominated by thoughts that exacerbate your negative feelings rather than soothe, you are likely to become flooded in response to your spouse's defensiveness, anger, stonewalling, etc. These negative feelings form a sort of feedback, creating symptoms of flooding like increased heart rate and flow of adrenaline, and the more your body feels flooded, the less able you are to soothe yourself and see the situation calmly. Instead, your thoughts and emotions contribute even more to your sense of being overwhelmed. Over time you become *conditioned* to look for and react to negatives in your spouse and your marriage. This becomes a self-fulfilling prophesy: the more you expect and search for negatives, the more likely you are to find them, and to highlight their significance in your mind.

THE DISTANCE AND ISOLATION CASCADE

If flooding goes on unabated, the results for a marriage are disastrous. Flooding is the driving force behind the final Distance and Isolation Cascade. This cascade is comprised of four stages that people seem to go through in withdrawing from a marriage.

FIRST STAGE: YOU SEE YOUR MARITAL PROBLEMS AS SEVERE.
Most couples would admit that their union is far from perfect, but once you perceive your problems as virtually impossible-to-fix obstacles, you've turned a dangerous corner. Has your marriage reached this unfortunate point?

SELF-TEST: HOW SEVERE IS THE PROBLEM?

This self-test is straightforward, to help you decide how severe you see your problems. Circle "yes" or "no" for the following statements:

1. My spouse and I have very severe communication problems.
     Yes   No

2. I have very little faith that we are going to be able to resolve our problems.
     Yes   No

3. The problems we have run very deep.
     Yes   No

4. Things have gotten so complex that I'm not sure there is a solution.
     Yes   No

5. Each of our problems has caused us a great deal of pain.
     Yes   No

6. I doubt whether we can reconcile our differences.
     Yes   No

7. It's going to be very hard for us to ever forgive one another for some of the hurt we have suffered.
     Yes   No

8. There is a great deal of intensity to our problems.
     Yes   No

9. We stand very little chance of ever having really good times together.
     Yes   No

10. There is very little respect in this relationship.
      Yes   No

11. I am not sure that we love each other.
      Yes   No

12. There are "wheels within wheels" to our problems—they are so difficult to solve.
    Yes   No

13. I have a sense of despair about our future together.
    Yes   No

14. Sometimes I feel bitter about how things have gotten between us.
    Yes   No

15. When it comes down to it, I am not sure I have very much hope.
    Yes   No

Scoring: If you answered "yes" to more than five of these questions, you have a very negative view of your marital difficulties. Most people who score at this level have unstable marriages that are either *hostile/engaged*, meaning there's a great deal of negativity but you still interact, or *hostile/detached*, meaning the hostility has reached such huge proportions that you avoid each other as much as possible (see chapter 3.) As long as you see your problems as severe, you may be stymied in your attempts to resolve them.

SECOND STAGE: TALKING THINGS OVER WITH YOUR SPOUSE SEEMS USELESS.

Not only do you perceive your marriage as very troubled but you also feel hopeless about being able to salvage it by communicating with your mate. Rather, you look for solutions on your own ("I'll try to be nicer to him," "I'll ignore her insults.") You may, for example, decide to avoid certain kinds of interactions with your spouse, or try to convince yourself that you're not upset by your spouse's actions when you really are. The following self-test will help you see whether your marriage has reached this stage.

SELF TEST: CAN YOU WORK THINGS OUT?

Answer "yes" or "no":

1. Talking things over with my partner only seems to make them worse.
   Yes   No

2. I'd rather just keep things to myself.
   Yes   No

3. I am a very private person about my feelings.
   Yes   No

4. When I'm in a bad mood I'd much rather just go off by myself.
   Yes   No

5. I don't see much point in discussing my troubles with my partner.
   Yes   No

6. Talking about our problems only gets them more muddled.
   Yes   No

7. There are some people you just can't talk to and my partner's one of those.
   Yes   No

8. I'd rather try to work out our marital problems alone.
   Yes   No

9. Our conversations about our problems never seem to get anywhere.
   Yes   No

10. I don't place a lot of faith in delving into my problems with my spouse.
    Yes   No

11. I have given up on trying to talk things out.
    Yes   No

12. I don't see any potential gain in trying to talk things over with my partner.
    Yes   No

Scoring: If you answered "yes" to four or more of these statements, you've given up on working things out with your spouse. This attitude almost inevitably leads to the next step in the Distance and Isolation Cascade.

THIRD STAGE: YOU START LEADING PARALLEL LIVES

We all know at least one couple like this—they occupy the same house but not the same universe. Think of Prince Charles and Princess Diana, even before they officially separated. Such marriages seem more like business arrangements than intimate relationships. Although the couple may live together, they rarely connect.

SELF-TEST: DO YOU LEAD PARALLEL LIVES?

Answer "yes" or "no":

1. We don't eat together as much as we used to.
   Yes   No

2. Sometimes it seems we are roommates rather than a married couple.
   Yes   No

3. We have fewer friends in common than we used to.
   Yes   No

4. We seem to do a lot more things separately.
   Yes   No

5. It seems that we have fewer and fewer interests in common.
   Yes   No

6. Sometimes we can go for quite a while without ever talking about our lives.
   Yes   No

7. Our lives are more parallel than connected.
   Yes   No

8. We often don't talk about how our separate days went.
   Yes   No

9. We don't spend very much time together anymore.
   Yes   No

10. We spend a lot of our free time apart.
    Yes   No

11. We don't set aside much time just to talk.
    Yes   No

12. I don't think that we know each other very well anymore.
    Yes   No

13. We don't have dinner together very much anymore.
    Yes   No

14. We rarely go out on dates together.
    Yes   No

15. A lot of our good times these days are with people other than each other.
    Yes   No

16. We seem to be avoiding each other.
    Yes   No

17. We are like two passing ships, going our separate ways.
    Yes   No

Scoring: If you answered "yes" to five or more of the statements, then you may well be leading parallel lives. Realizing that the situation has deteriorated to this extreme is the first step toward rediscovering each other.

FOURTH STAGE: LONELINESS

Officially, you are still married. But you feel so isolated that there's little difference between your marriage and living alone. Loneliness is one of the most painful human conditions. There's a tragic irony in feeling this way in a marriage, which is supposed to offer love and companionship. People who reach this point don't necessarily divorce. But unless they seek each other out, and in most cases get professional help, the marriage is for all intents over. Again, the questions may seem obvious, but this test can clarify your sense of just how lonely you are.

SELF-TEST: HOW LONELY IS YOUR MARRIAGE?

Answer "yes" or "no":

1. Marriage is a lot lonelier than I thought it would be.
   Yes   No

2. We're not as close as I wish we were.
   Yes   No

3. I feel an emptiness in this marriage.
   Yes   No

4. I often feel bored when we do things together.
   Yes   No

5. I feel very restless and sad even when we're together.
   Yes   No

6. Lots of times I don't know what to do with myself.
   Yes   No

7. At times I feel bored and restless in this marriage.
   Yes   No

8. I long for someone I can be close to.
   Yes   No

9. I feel so lonely it hurts.
   Yes   No

10. Something is missing from my marriage.
    Yes   No

11. I wish people would call me more often.
    Yes   No

12. I often wish I had someone to be with.
    Yes   No

13. I don't feel that I'm an important part of someone's life.
    Yes   No

14. I don't feel that I belong to anyone.
    Yes   No

15. I often feel emotionally isolated.
    Yes   No

16. I feel abandoned in this marriage.
    Yes   No

17. There is no one I can turn to.
    Yes   No

18. I often feel left out.
    Yes   No

19. No one knows me.
    Yes   No

20. No one understands me.
    Yes   No

21. There is often no one I can talk to.
    Yes   No

22. I often feel a great need for companionship.
    Yes   No

23. I have become very withdrawn in this marriage.
    Yes   No

24. I feel disconnected.
    Yes   No

If you answered "yes" to eight or more of the questions, you may have reached the end of the Distance and Isolation Cascade. Feeling lonely in marriage makes you vulnerable to having an affair, if this hasn't already occurred. Research suggests that it also makes you more likely to become ill, especially if you are male. The first step toward finding each other again is to admit to your spouse how you're feeling. Simple admissions like "I miss you," "I feel needy all the time," or "This is a dangerous situation for our marriage and my health" can start you on the journey back. You'll find more detailed information on undoing the damage wrought by the Distance and Isolation Cascade in chapters 7 and 8.

REWRITING HISTORY

Even after reading this far, you may not have a clear sense of whether your marriage is teetering on the brink. There is one more important bit of evidence that can help you assess where you stand. Through my research on couples I have found that nothing foretells a marriage's future as accurately as how a couple retells their past. The crucial factor is not necessarily the *reality* of a marriage's early days but how husband and wife currently view their joint history.

Why does a marriage's history so often offer clues to its future? Quite simply, when a marriage is unraveling, we found that husband and wife come to recast their earlier times together in a negative light. Your recall of previous disappointments and slights becomes dramatically enhanced. Where once you might have looked back fondly on your first dance together or buying your wedding rings, now you focus on the jarring notes that seemed to foreshadow your current dissatisfactions—your fiancé showing up tipsy or the late-night argument over the wording of the invitations. The key point is that putting a negative spin on your past is an early warning sign that your marriage is in trouble. Rewriting history may begin *well before you become aware that your marriage is in serious danger.* That's why it's so helpful to be aware of how you view your marital history.

The value of this knowledge became apparent to me after my team completed a long-term study of fifty-six couples. We asked these couples a number of questions related to their marriage's history, including how they met, courted, and wed, their past tough times and how they got over them, what the good times were (and what they are today). When first interviewed, none of the couples had plans to separate. But three years later, we found that seven couples out of the forty-seven we were able to locate had indeed divorced. And 100 percent of the time we were able to predict which couples these were based solely on how they had answered our questions about their marriage's history three years earlier! Also, for the forty couples who stayed together we had predicted that positive outcome in thirty-seven, or 93 percent, of them. Our overall accuracy in predicting marital outcome was 94 percent.

Keep in mind that this was a preliminary study. Still, these intriguing results strongly suggest a link between how you perceive your marital history and your likely future. At first glance, you may think that there's an obvious and simple explanation for our findings: some couples have negative memories because their earlier years really weren't very pleasant—a sign that they were wrong for each other from the start. If that's the case, why should it be a remarkable discovery that they ended up divorcing? While this may be true for some of the marriages we studied, the total number who put a negative skew on the past was far higher than can be accounted for in this way. After all, most people view courtship and weddings as joyful times, even if stressful.

Although the current divorce rate for new marriages is estimated at between 50 percent and 67 percent, certainly far more than half of couples walk down the aisle feeling optimistic and hopeful. Only later, when they are faced with what seem to be unsolvable conflicts, did they start recasting the past in such dark colors. People who are feeling distressed more easily remember negative episodes from the past—so your current negativity triggers negative memories that reinforce your current feeling. That's why this recasting is such an accurate warning sign that a marriage is headed for deep trouble.

I believe that there are a handful of specific factors related to how couples recall their past that may cumulatively predict their future. The most important of these factors are:

Chaos vs. a Sense of Control. Couples who later divorced tended to look back on their early days as a time of great confusion, uncertainty, and anxiety. Whatever the reality, they viewed their coming together as a stressful, almost haphazard occurrence, rather than one motivated by commitment and joy. Consider the contrast in the memories of Dexter and Midge, a couple who are still happily married, with Jewel and Anthony, who ended up divorcing.

INTERVIEWER: Do you remember deciding to get married?

DEXTER: We waited far longer than I wanted to get married. We were looking forward to it.

MIDGE: We got to the point where we just knew it was right. There was no question—we didn't want to be apart.

JEWEL: Yeah, he was yelling at me and asked me if I'd marry him and I said yes . . . we were fighting. I guess we had been dating each other so steadily that marriage seemed natural, the next step.

ANTHONY: I wasn't conscious of deciding to get married. I was in kind of a blind panic after the wedding was over.

Couples who recall their early days as chaotic often say that external events controlled their lives. For example, a couple may recall that they got married for financial reasons, or because of a pregnancy.

Disappointment vs. Glorifying the Struggle. All marriages go through hard times. But some couples look back at their earlier difficulties with pride that they were able to surmount the obstacles together. Others seem dragged down by the crises and feel that their early days were a time of disillusionment. Dwayne and Rita, another couple who later divorced, expressed this perfectly:

DWAYNE: People told us when we were going to get married, "Oh your first year is going to be rough." And we said, "Oh no, we love each other." We thought everything would be just great and dandy.

RITA: Yeah, we thought, "We love each other; we won't have these conflicts. Love conquers all." Well, it doesn't. Getting married was like, "welcome to the real world." It really took us by surprise. The first few months were really hard; we didn't expect that.

DWAYNE: Marriage wasn't as special as I thought it would be. I thought more things would stand out.

RITA: Yeah, I thought there would be more excitement.

Not surprisingly, Jewel and Anthony expressed similar sentiments:

JEWEL: There were a lot of downs.

ANTHONY: A lot of things went wrong but I don't remember what they were.

JEWEL: The whole year was a travesty.

ANTHONY: We seemed to spend all our time trying to pick up the pieces.

By contrast, Dexter and Midge recalled their past troubles with much fondness, humor, and even a sense of triumph:

MIDGE: Did you ever see the "Odd Couple"? Felix Unger over here. That first year, we drove each other crazy.

DEXTER: Midge was very unorganized and untidy and I was the opposite.

MIDGE: Direct opposites!

DEXTER: I'd say we're in the middle of the line now.

MIDGE: It was hard at first but we both really felt that our commitment to each other was forever. We knew it was gonna work; we proved that we could make it through the rough spots of the year.

If the first two couples were not currently trapped in the marital rapids, their memories might very well have the same flavor as Midge and Dexter's. The significant factor is not how difficult their early married life was by objective standards but their current attitude toward those days.

The other three factors that are important clues to future divorce concern the husband more than the wife. This may be because, in general, men tend to display signs of marital distress earlier and more intensely than do women. Therefore, they may be more intent on rewriting history.

We-ness vs. *Separate Lives.* The more the husband framed his marital history as a joint undertaking, the more likely the couple was to remain happily married in the future. For example, when Dexter was asked about his adjustments to marrying Midge, his sense of connection with her was apparent:

DEXTER: When we moved in we kept the house together, we handled the money together, everything. We shared cooking, cleaning.

MIDGE: There's never been a time when I've had a problem and thought, "Well, this is my problem, I'll take care of it." We've always divvied them up.

But Anthony didn't express that sense of bonding when he explored his past with Jewel. Instead, he recalled how distant he felt:

ANTHONY: We attempted to find common interests; it just never worked. (*Turning to Jewel*) What in the hell did we get married for?

Expansiveness. It was also a healthy sign if the husband remembered specifics about how he felt about his future wife and their courtship. It was a bad sign if he didn't. Compare how Dexter and Anthony answered the question: "How did you decide this was the person you were going to marry?"

DEXTER: Midge had the qualities I was looking for, she carried herself well, and she was attractive. I didn't see myself looking for anything else. That's what I was looking for, and I'd found it, so it was really just cut and dry.

ANTHONY: The height was right, the weight was right, I like tall women.

INTERVIEWER: Anything else that struck you about her?

ANTHONY: No, I don't tend to pay a lot of attention to my surroundings.

While Dexter could probably go on and on about his feelings for Midge, Anthony is hard put to recall any specifics about Jewel at all.

Though he claims he's just inattentive, his lack of responsiveness is a clear sign that he has distanced himself from his marriage and has reshaped his view of the past to fit his current attitude.

Affection. Husbands in stable marriages tended to speak about their wives fondly, to take pride in them. In marriages that would later fail, husbands didn't express these positive feelings:

> INTERVIEWER: Do you remember your wedding?
>
> DEXTER: Oh yes, loved it. Never had so much fun in all my life. It was super. Midge has never been so pretty as she was when she walked down the aisle in her white dress.

> INTERVIEWER: What did you think of your wife at first?
>
> ANTHONY: She struck me as not having a whole lot of common sense. I don't know, I don't know. When I think back about it, I really don't know.

You'd hardly need to be an experienced marriage counselor to conclude from these memories that Anthony and Jewel's marriage was in serious trouble at the time they were interviewed, whereas Dexter and Midge's was very stable. Yet it can be harder to see your own marriage so clearly. If you're trying to sort out how you currently view your marriage's past and present, the following two-part test can help.

SELF-TEST: TELLING YOUR STORY

Answer "yes" or "no" to all questions in Part A and Part B.

● *Part A* ●

1. I am genuinely fond of my partner.
   Yes   No

2. I can easily speak of the good times in our marriage.
   Yes   No

3. I can easily remember romantic, special times in our marriage.
   Yes   No

4. I am physically attracted to my spouse.
   Yes   No

5. My partner has some specific qualities that make me proud.
   Yes   No

6. I feel a genuine sense of "we" as opposed to "I" in this marriage.
   Yes   No

7. We have the same general beliefs and values.
   Yes   No

8. My spouse is my best friend.
   Yes   No

9. I get lots of support in my marriage.
   Yes   No

10. My home is a place to come to get support and reduce stress.
    Yes   No

11. I can easily recall when we first met, the marriage proposal, and our wedding.
    Yes   No

12. We divide up household chores in a fair way.
    Yes   No

13. We have planned things out and have had a sense of control over our lives together.
    Yes   No

14. I am proud of this marriage.
    Yes   No

15. There are things I don't like about my partner, but I can live with them.
    Yes   No

16. Marriage is a struggle, but it's been worth it.
    Yes   No

A. TOTAL NUMBER OF ITEMS CHECKED "YES":

● *Part B* ●

1. I feel cynical about my marriage.
   Yes   No

2. When I think of my own marriage, I can think of lots of sarcastic things to say about the institution of marriage.

        Yes   No

3. I have a lot of criticisms of my partner.

        Yes   No

4. Our lives are very separate.

        Yes   No

5. Our beliefs and values are very different.

        Yes   No

6. I don't think of this marriage as a "we."

        Yes   No

7. I don't really have a sense of trust in my partner.

        Yes   No

8. The stresses of my life just get added to at home.

        Yes   No

9. I have only vague memories of our first meeting, the marriage proposal, and our wedding.

        Yes   No

10. It seems like problems have beset this marriage throughout.

        Yes   No

11. It seems like we have had very little control over our lives.

        Yes   No

12. I feel disillusioned and disappointed in my marriage.

        Yes   No

13. Marriage is not what I thought it would be.

        Yes   No

14. My partner's faults are basically unacceptable to me.

        Yes   No

15. Things are very unequal in this marriage.

        Yes   No

16. When you come down to it, my marital struggles have been pretty meaningless.

        Yes   No

B. TOTAL NUMBER OF ITEMS CHECKED "YES":

Scoring: Subtract your total score for Part B from your total score for Part A. If your final score is six or above, this suggests that you have a mostly positive view of your marital history. That's an excellent sign for your relationship's prospects. See chapter 8 for advice on continuing to nurture your marriage to keep it thriving and to avoid future problems.

If your score is lower than six, it's clear your feelings of admiration, fondness, and solidarity with your spouse have dwindled to dangerous levels. Remember that how you view your history together may be the most powerful predictor of your marriage's future. See chapter 7 for advice on talking this over with your spouse. Thinking back together about your initial positive feelings toward each other can provide the hope you need to work toward regaining that connection now.

NOW WHAT?

Much of my research on marriage has attempted to solve the mystery of why positivity triumphs in some marriages while negativity overruns others. When two couples start out equally in love and optimistic about the future, why do their paths diverge so dramatically? For one couple the promise turns to despair as they watch their marriage be consumed by chaos, loneliness, mistrust, and hopelessness. They feel under attack by their spouse and think of him or her as the enemy. They even recast their past to fit this new, sad reality. The other couple finds that their interest and involvement in each other deepens over the years, as does their fondness, hope, affection, admiration, and sense of commitment and togetherness. When this couple looks back on their past, they glorify it—even times of struggle are now viewed as triumphs.

The key to these couples' disparate fates, I believe, is not necessarily that one couple started off more compatible than the other. Yet somehow the happy couple learned to navigate expertly through the rocky times that any marriage encounters. Because of that, the four horsemen never overrode their relationship and they were able to avoid barreling down the marital cascades. As a result, they never lost the 5-to-1 ratio in favor of the positive that keeps a couple stable, whether they settle into a volatile, hostile, or avoidant style.

All of this suggests that there is hope even for couples who are in despair over the state of their marriage. By understanding why distance has grown between you and your spouse, you can begin to recover the goodness that exists under all of the layers of hurt, misunderstanding, and loneliness. The following chapters offer advice on how to salvage your marriage. The first step is to understand the different histories and needs that men and women usually bring to an intimate relationship. The next is to communicate with love and understanding during the bad times—and then to keep working together even after your marriage improves.

FIVE

THE TWO MARRIAGES:
HIS AND HERS

In a scene from the movie *Sweet Dreams*, country-western singer Patsy Cline has just returned home from a successful performance. She is in high spirits, energized by the enthusiasm of her fans, and, naturally, she wants to share her excitement with her husband, Gerald. Having spent the evening at home working on his model ship, Gerald is caught up in his own world. He asks Patsy, "How'd it go?" twice, without bothering to listen to her answer. Finally, she confronts him directly and asks whether he wanted to talk with her or not. When he looks up, she is glowering. But Gerald doesn't have a clue why Patsy is so angry.

This classic marital impasse is all too common—a wife seeking emotional connection from a withdrawn husband. Do you recognize this pattern in your own marriage? In Patsy and Gerald's case, it leads to a painful, vicious cycle. The more he withdraws, the more frustrated Patsy becomes. "I can't stand it," she tells her mother. "It makes me want to scream and claw my face."

By now you probably have a clear idea of how marriages can slide from good to bad to worse to divorce. But there remains one crucial force behind this marital cascade that we haven't yet explored: the dramatic and fundamental differences between men and women. For complex reasons, rooted in a combination of biology and socialization, the genders tend to view the world of relationships very differently. Just like Patsy and her husband, men and women often "miss" each other, resulting in two marriages: his and hers.

I find very common patterns in how the sexes interact in marriage. But keep in mind that these findings do not apply to everybody. Generalizations are always dangerous because they are just that: general. So remember that what I describe here is not true of all men and women—and may not be true of you and your spouse. You'll find this chapter helpful to the extent that you recognize yourself and your husband or wife in what follows.

Let's begin with the widely held belief that women are more comfortable in intimate relationships—that they can easily swim in an ocean of intense emotions while men are more likely to feel "lost at sea." I have seen this assumption hold true over and over again.

Can you remember the last time you and your spouse discussed a problem in your relationship? Who brought up the hot topic? I'd be willing to bet it was the woman. Though traditionally described as less assertive in the world at large, in marital relationships women tend to be the emotional managers. They are usually better attuned than men to the changing emotional climate in their relationships and more willing to confront problems. Like Patsy Cline, it's usually the wife who insists that issues get talked about, while the husband tries to avoid talking. This confront-avoid pattern between spouses typically goes something like this:

WIFE: (*Worried voice*) Is something wrong?

HUSBAND: (*Distant voice*) Nope. Not a thing.

WIFE: I can tell that you're annoyed at me—I can see it in your face. What's wrong?

HUSBAND: (*Sounding annoyed*) I already told you, there's nothing wrong. Will you lay off me? I just need some time to myself.

WIFE: Are you angry because I was talking on the phone with Margie during supper? Or because I made that date with the Wilsons on

Saturday without asking you first? I thought for sure you'd want to go.

HUSBAND: (*Looking away*) I already told you, there's nothing wrong!

Men are by and large reluctant to dive head first into emotional issues. But why? Much of the answer seems to lie in the vast gulf between what men and women learn about intimacy as children. In a nutshell, boys typically are not taught the skills necessary to navigate through the shifting emotional tides of an intimate relationship while girls are given intense schooling on the subject. Like a person thrown overboard without first being taught how to swim, the average man is understandably fearful of drowning in the same whirlpool of emotions that a woman easily glides through every day. Add to this some compelling evidence that men also have a stronger physiological reaction to certain emotions than do women and it becomes easy to understand why the world of feelings is by and large outside most mens' comfort zone.

These gender differences help clarify why men are so much more likely than women to be stonewallers, withdrawing when their wife confronts them. As we have seen, stonewalling is the most destructive of the four horsemen leading to a marriage's downfall. The fundamental emotional differences between the sexes also help explain why there are certain common areas of conflict in most marriages: namely, how often the couple has sex and who does how much housework and child care.

But research into what men and women bring to their marriages points to good news as well: There are specific actions you can take to ensure that your differences enrich rather than harm your relationship. The first and most essential step is to understand where the dissimilarities between men and women originate. Like most emotional patterns, the roots of marital discord may be found in childhood.

BOYS AND GIRLS: SEPARATE UNIVERSES

For a firsthand look at why husbands and wives often have so much trouble relating, you may only need to recall your own childhood. Or, if your memory is fuzzy, simply watch youngsters at play.

The way you interacted with your playground friends can strongly affect how well you communicate with your marriage partner today. The reason: the playground behavior of boys and girls has always been, and still is, vastly different. In fact, our upbringing couldn't be a *worse* training ground for a successful marriage.

The first problem for future marriages arises in preschool when boys and girls begin to play separately. You can often hear little boys on the playground taunting girls, "Go away. This is a *boys' game*. We hate girls." And girls—even when they are building with blocks rather than playing house—want to get rid of boys. "Leave us alone. Boys are gross," they squeal in horror whenever a boy tries to interrupt or join them. Sex segregation is less common when children are *very* young, but becomes standard toward middle childhood, reaching a zenith at about age seven. In a door-to-door survey, we found that 36 percent of preschoolers said they had playmates of the opposite sex. By kindergarten, only 23 percent still did. And by second grade such friendships were almost nonexistent. In elementary school, even if the teacher forces boy-girl pairs to work together on class projects, you will almost always see same-sex groupings during recess or in the cafeteria when the kids get to choose their own playmates. Because of this preference, boys and girls grow up in parallel universes where most of the emotional rules are different. This may be where the trouble between the sexes begins.

Why do children voluntarily segregate themselves by gender? The tendency may be partly biological in origin. Boys are more aggressive. Universally they love rough-and-tumble play, wrestling, climbing, running, unrestrained movements, loud noise, play that involves competition, and run-and-chase games that require large spaces and lots of children. Girls usually prefer quieter games—dolls, dress-up, jacks, hopscotch, jump rope, house—which they tend to play in small groups close to the school building. Girls typically see boys as annoying, noisy creatures, while boys see the way girls play as just plain boring.

The preference for associating with members of one's own sex continues well into young adulthood. Of course, boys and girls get attracted to each other during the teenage years. Many date, go steady, and have passionate sexual relationships. And yet, a girl's best girl-friends and a boy's best buddies are usually the deepest, most significant, and longest-lasting relationships formed during this period.

This avoidance between the genders from the early school years until young adulthood can have disastrous consequences when love finally blooms. After all, how can a man and woman be expected to easily form and maintain a lifelong romance after a childhood of virtual segregation? It's almost as unrealistic as expecting a visiting Martian to know how to commune intimately with an Earthling.

I remember when I first started dating at age 14, I had read somewhere that the purpose of a date was "to entertain girls." So I went to the library and took out a book called *500 Successful Jokes* and memorized as many as I could before Saturday night. When I picked up my date, I immediately started in with, "Did you hear the joke about? . . ." I went on and on, telling her joke after joke. That poor girl! I had no idea how to have a real conversation with her. It didn't even occur to me that I could talk to a girl about the same things I discussed with my male friends. It was truly as if this girl and I were from different planets!

THE ACTIVITY VS. THE RELATIONSHIP

Even if boys and girls did play more closely together as children (as some do), a wide gulf would still remain between them by the teen years and beyond. This is because they tend to have very different emotional communication styles from early on. You can see this disparity in what children consider important when they are playing. Usually, boys care most about *the game*, while girls care most about *the relationship* between the players. There's a saying that goes, "Boys play team sports in order to compete, and girls compete in order to be on a team." Despite the recent emphasis on athletic competition for girls, this still seems to hold true.

Have you ever noticed that boys don't let quarrels break up the all-important game? It's not that they don't get angry—boys quarrel all the time on the ball field, arguing endlessly over the rules—but they just don't seem to attach the same importance that girls do to their arguments. In the most intense debates during boys' games, the final word is almost always to "play it over." The goal is to literally "keep the ball in play," to not let emotions rule. This holds true from Little League up to the highest level of professional athletics. When watching sports on television, I often observe grown-up players acting just like preschool boys—screaming at each other, fighting, and calling names. Yet, a few minutes later, after being penalized by the referee, the players return and continue playing as if nothing of great significance has happened. They don't let bad feelings stop the action. The bottom line is that for males, the game itself, with its focus on teamwork, competition, and accomplishment, is what's important—not how the individual players relate or feel.

There is certainly a positive side to this emotional management. At times it does make sense to subordinate feelings to getting a job done. But in the realm of marriage, a man's tendency to contain uncomfortable emotions—and avoid his wife's—becomes a decided handicap.

A woman's very different approach to emotions has its roots in how little girls like to play. In contrast to boys, among girls the eruption of a dispute tends to end a game. That's because the object of playing a game like hopscotch for most girls is not winning so much as interacting with each other. Hopscotch is an excuse for talking and sharing feelings. If a game stops, there are usually tears, threats such as, "I won't be your friend anymore," and counterthreats, pouting, talking it through, and, if all goes well, making up.

The dissimilar emotional lessons men and women learn in childhood may be most clearly seen in how parents respond when boys and girls cry. Despite new parenting attitudes, boys still get teased in the playground if they shed tears. Even if the parents have encouraged their son to express his feelings throughout his early childhood, once he's in school his peer group's approval matters to him most. During midchildhood, from about eight to twelve, expressing emotion is considered terribly "uncool" for both genders, but particularly for boys. Very quickly, boys are trained to hide their feelings behind a mask of apparent indifference while girls are left much more leeway. If a girl gets hurt and cries during a game, she quickly becomes the center of a concerned and supportive group of her female teammates. If a young boy is hurt during a game, you will see him squeezing his facial muscles and fists as hard as he can to hold back his tears. If he loses his cool, he will probably be teased by his friends, unless the injury is serious. A boy who cries often will be scorned and mocked mercilessly. Because "crybaby," and "wimp" are the worst labels males can get stuck with during childhood, boys soon realize that the ultimate trick is not to respond emotionally, *no matter what.*

This repression can be reinforced by training well into adolescence. A scene from the movie, *Dead Poet's Society,* shows how a teenage boy, Neil, is conditioned by his Dad to hide all of his normal feelings. Emotions are forbidden territory in a male world where achievement and competition are the only goals. Neil's father insists that Neil should go to Harvard and become a physician. Neil argues passionately that he doesn't want to be a doctor, but his father responds by telling him not to be so dramatic. Neil, who really wants to be an actor, replies, "I've got to tell you what I feel!" His dad refuses to listen and replies sarcastically, "Tell me what you feel! What is it?" Neil, looking terrified, remains quiet. Finally, Neil mutters, "Nothing." He does the correct thing in his family—he buries his feelings. The father leaves the room, satisfied that Neil has finally said the only right thing in this situation—*nothing.*

Another prime example of the strikingly different way young boys and girls address emotional issues during playtime is how they incorporate danger into their games. By age four, "boy talk" often entails discussing adventures and ways to master the environment. If boys become scared by something, they deal with the fear by trying to overcome it in fantasy or play, or joke about it. In contrast, when girls become frightened they comfort one another and discuss their feelings.

Young boys rarely ever say, "I'm really scared." Instead, they come up with ways of feeling a sense of mastery over the rather scary external world. Young girls cope with the fear in an entirely different way than boys. They encourage each other to express their anxieties directly and then take a parental, comforting role, soothing it away with words of love, loyalty, and affection.

From early childhood, boys learn to suppress their emotions while girls learn to express and manage the complete range of feelings. Small wonder that by the time they grow up, meet, and marry, men and women are so often at opposite ends of the spectrum when it comes to the importance they place on expressing feelings. A man is more likely to equate being emotional with weakness and vulnerability because he has been raised to *do* rather than to voice what he feels. Meanwhile, women have spent their early years learning how to verbalize all kinds of emotions.

Ideally, through marriage men and women learn from each other's strengths—a wife can help guide her husband toward accepting and expressing his feelings while a husband can help his wife see the benefits of action and "keeping the ball in play," which her upbringing may not have emphasized. But sometimes, the differences between men and women become a bane rather than a benefit in marriage. When a woman looks for the same intimacy with her husband that she has experienced with female friends, she may be sorely disappointed. Likewise, a man who hopes to duplicate his "buddy" relationships with his wife may feel overwhelmed by her need to talk about feelings or for emotional intimacy. Finding she demands more intensity than he can comfortably offer, he may withdraw. In a happy marriage, a couple can usually sort out these differences. But in an unstable marriage where negativity has the upper hand, these two emotional styles can clash wildly, feeding the four horsemen.

BIOLOGICAL ROOTS

The vast difference in the childhood experiences of men and women is not the only reason that the genders tend to have such divergent emotional styles. I believe much of the disparity may be caused by certain fundamental biological differences and how our society *responds* to them. In other words, it's my belief that marital strife has a physiological basis as well as a psychological one. In order to fully understand why husbands and wives so often miss each other's needs, we have to recognize that the sexes may be physically programmed to react differently to emotional conflict—beginning in childhood.

For example, next time you're at the supermarket look around to see which toddlers are throwing tantrums. Chances are that more of the flying fists and feet will belong to boys rather than girls. Temper tantrums and controlling emotions are issues for all young children to varying degrees. But in a study where parents were asked to keep track of their children's tantrums, young boys had far more and longer-lasting tantrums than girls. The reason, it seems, is that boys have greater trouble than girls recovering from strong upsets like sadness and anger. Perhaps because it is more difficult for young boys to control their natural aggressive feelings, they get many more messages than do girls that emotional expression is bad.

For example, when three-year-old Alex was told that he had to go home from the playground, he fell to the ground screaming and kicking. Ten minutes later, his frustrated mom carried him to the car. Struggling against his wild punching, she barely managed to strap Alex into his car seat. His face bright red, his voice raspy from screaming, he continued kicking and yelling even after they arrived home and he was put in a "time-out" for five minutes. He kept banging on the door of his bedroom, screaming bloody murder at the top of his lungs. He sounded so miserable that his mother worried that the new neighbors would assume she was beating him up. His time-out was extended five more minutes. Finally exhausted, Alex calmed down enough to go on with his day. What did Alex learn from this experience? Because it was extremely hard for him to let go of his negative feelings, he received a great deal of disciplining from his mother, which told him that she disapproved of his behavior.

By contrast, three-year-old Anjali also protested when her mother told her it was time to leave the swings. Anjali cried, yelled, and stamped her feet. She called her mother "a stupid mom," and had to be carried to the car just like Alex. But by the time the car was out of the parking lot, Anjali was already singing along with the *Peter Pan* tape on her tape player. "I won't grow up," she crooned happily. Unlike Alex, she did not need even one "time-out" when she got home— and so experienced less disapproval from her mother.

This is the key emotional difference between men and women: men grow up having a harder time recovering from upset, being told to suppress feelings, and learning to avoid them. But women recover more easily, were encouraged to value expressing feelings, and learned to express and explore them.

MEN AND FLOODING

Just like little Alex in the playground, men tend to have shorter fuses and longer-lasting explosions than women, leaving them more vulnerable to stress. We've seen this in our own laboratory: during difficult marital discussions, a man's blood pressure and heart rate will rise much higher and will stay elevated longer than his wife's.

To see how much more readily men are flooded than women, consider the differences in Kirk and Agnes's heart rates as they discuss one of their major conflict areas—her tendency to yell at their two young daughters more than he would like. Before the conversation starts, both of their heart rates are in the normal range—his is 75 beats per minute and hers is 62.3 beats per minute. But as Kirk begins to tell Agnes of his concerns, his heart rate quickly skyrockets in anticipation of her reaction.

> KIRK: If you don't like it when the kids get angry and lose their temper, you can't hope to correct it at all by giving them the example that it's okay to lose your temper and yell, and that sort of thing. [His heart rate is 95.7.]

> AGNES: I'm not saying it's okay to give them that example. But sometimes, it's like what happens to teachers—the kids push them too far and they yell at them because you don't get any reaction if you just talk to them. Sometimes you have to raise your voice. You know, I wish I didn't raise my voice like I did. I wish I were more like you. [Her heart rate is 62.3.]

> KIRK: (*Sighs.*) [His heart rate is 95.7.]

> AGNES: But I don't think my yelling is why our kids throw temper tantrums when they don't like the color of their socks.

> KIRK: I think sometimes you can just let 'em know there's no choice in the matter without, uh, yelling at them and letting the whole thing break down.

> AGNES: Well, to me, I don't think our kids are made to accept our authority enough. I notice you'll let them argue and argue and argue with you and you'll try to convince them. I guess I'm a firm believer in, with a five-year-old and three-year-old, "If I said that's the way it is, then that's the way it is." [Heart rate: 56.1.]

> KIRK: (*Swallows.*) [Heart rate: 86.6.]

It makes a crucial difference that Kirk's heart rate immediately rose to a very fast rate and took a long time to recover: the physiological arousal itself made it very difficult for him to listen to Agnes. His high heart rates during their discussion also meant that he was probably secreting a lot of adrenaline, contributing to his eventually becoming very withdrawn, and finally stonewalling.

There are two primary explanations for these physiological differences between the sexes. First, the male's autonomic nervous system, which controls much of the body's stress response, may be more sensitive and take far longer to recover from emotional upset than does the average female's. I'm not implying that women are "invulnerable" to marital stress, but that compared with men it may take more intense conflict before women experience its harmful effects. This may explain why women are so much readier than men to dive directly into potentially explosive issues.

Second, men may be more reactive because even when they withdraw from an argument they are more likely to repeat negative thoughts that keep them riled up. If you could read their minds, you might hear phrases like, "I don't have to take this crap," or "It's all her fault," or "I'll get her back for this." Such inner scripts, whether of righteous indignation or innocent victimization, are clearly not self-soothing. Compared with a woman, it seems to be much harder for a man to relax his guard and say, "Honey, let's talk about it."

The most disastrous result of these physiological differences for marriage is that men are far more likely than women to be stone-wallers—and *destructive* stonewallers—when tension builds. The male tendency to stonewall is hardly surprising. We have found repeatedly that men get flooded far faster during a tense marital exchange than do their wives. In fact, it often takes only the arrival of the first horseman—criticism—to flood men. For women, it usually takes at least contempt, the second horseman, to cause severe distress. Since men are more biologically reactive to stress, they are more likely to need to protect themselves by withdrawing. Add to that the lesson learned over and over again in boyhood that they should suppress their aggression and anxiety and it's no wonder that 85 percent of stone-wallers are men. If this is true of your marriage, you are not alone.

Although stonewalling may protect a man from stress, it *creates* enormous stress in his wife, as you may have found. Let's go back to the disagreement between Kirk and Agnes about disciplining the kids. As Kirk continues to complain about Agnes's child-rearing habits she begins to feel attacked by him. She tells him so, which leads him to stonewall. Now she is in tears.

AGNES: (*Crying*) Well, honey, I say all the time I need to work on not yelling so much. But I don't see why *you* never say, "Okay, I'll try to do things differently too." It's always just my fault. And I always end up saying I'll try harder.

KIRK: (*Smacks lips*) Any other comments to make? [Long pause while he stonewalls and Agnes looks at him, still crying.]

AGNES: No, not really. [His heart rate during stonewalling was 84.4. Her heart rate during his stonewalling was 90.]

It took Kirk's stonewalling to finally elevate Agnes's heart rate above normal. A man's stonewalling tends to trigger a stress reaction in both him and his wife, but for very different reasons. A man's upset is probably due to the tape of distress-maintaining thoughts that runs through his head while he sits there silently. But this stonewalling is painful to the wife, because she views it as disapproval and rejection. Accustomed to working through emotional problems with her female friends, the wife is likely to find her husband's withdrawal devastating, infuriating, and inexplicable.

Do you remember this phrase from the 1970s hit song: "People who need people are the luckiest people in the world?" The truth is that men don't seem to have nearly as much need to relate to others as women do. Men avoid emotional conflicts by going off by themselves, and as long as the withdrawal doesn't lead to prolonged periods of loneliness, they usually feel just fine about it. Whether he goes to his woodshop, plays computer games, jogs, or just drives around, the man's main purpose is to escape the emotional roller-coaster. It's a self-protective act. If you ask a male stonewaller to describe his state of mind, he often says, "I'm trying not to react." He feels like he's idling in neutral even though his wife perceives his silence as an act of hostility.

On the other hand, if you are a wife who stonewalls (there are some!) you probably do not cause your husband much physical distress. Like most men, he is probably rather relieved, in fact, when you withdraw from emotional confrontations. At least he knows he won't be attacked, and, after all, withdrawal and avoidance are reactions men understand very well. Additionally, if you are like most female stonewallers, you tend to focus on self-soothing thoughts while you withdraw, such as, "I really do love him," "I'm sorry he's really upset now," "I don't have to take his anger personally," "This is really a good marriage, he's just in a bad mood because of his job," or, "Just relax, it will get better." With such positive self-talk, it's not surprising that stonewalling women are able to forgive more easily than men after a period of withdrawal—making it a bit easier on both of them.

However, no matter who does the stonewalling, the issues being discussed remain unresolved. After all, you can't solve marital problems if your spouse "isn't home."

BALANCING THE SHIP OF MARRIAGE

In general, it may be more desirable biologically for women to get issues aired and settled and for men to avoid them. Thus, you probably find you and your spouse have somewhat incompatible approaches to dealing with your marital problems, even if you are firmly ensconced in a stable marriage. Even in good marriages, there's always a degree of inequity, with the woman typically the couple's emotional captain. She's at the helm of the relation-ship, reading the emotional weather moment by moment and deciding whether to head straight into a storm or to reroute the boat. If you play that role, your husband probably chooses to ride out the inevitable storms down below, listening to baseball games on his shortwave, while you want to be confrontational. Your husband is more likely to be rational and placating, and to minimize problems even if he doesn't withdraw from them. And if your relation-ship begins to sink under the stress of an unhappy marriage, these gender differences can become exaggerated, making matters much worse.

In fact, we find that, by and large, in happy marriages there are *no* gender differences in emotional expression! But in unhappy marriages all the gender differences we've been talking about emerge: Men are more defensive; men try to keep the emotion on a neutral track but women don't; men are the big stonewallers, withdrawing from the negative emotions of their wives because they are more easily flooded. And the men's withdrawal and defensiveness just fan the flames of their wives' frustration.

There are several ways that these differences between men and women can propel a tumble down the marital rapids. Here's a summary of the most common gender-related problems I've seen in marriages. You can go over these descriptions with your spouse and see if any of them fit your partnership.

Husbands and wives tend to have different and very specific grievances as the marital cascades get underway. Husbands gripe about their wives' complaining, criticizing, and emotionality. They say such things as, "My wife is a nag," or "My wife is quick tempered." Wives' grievances mainly concern their husbands' emotional withdrawal, saying, "He doesn't talk things over," or, "I just can't figure him out."

Men are more likely to be "too rational" and downplay emotions. They may not even recognize when an issue has an emotional cause and solution, rather than an expedient, practical one. For example, in the movie *Terms of Endearment,* a scene between Aurora and Garrett illustrates the mutual discomfort produced by women's desire to express emotion and men's tendency to avoid it, even if it's positive. Aurora has just told Garrett that she loves him. He hasn't responded, so she asks him if he's had any reaction to her avowal of love. Not realizing how difficult it might be for her to ask him this question, Garrett jokes back, saying, "I don't know what to say, except my stock answer." Aurora asks him what this might be. He replies, "I love you too, kid,"—an answer that hurts her, because it's "stock" rather than his heartfelt feeling about her.

Women are more likely to complain about and criticize their spouse. It's usually the wife who brings in the first horseman, criticism (though both partners are equally likely to be contemptuous or defensive). For example, Greg was making dinner for his family. His wife, Peggy, was unable to let him do it completely "on his own," feeling that she had to oversee his every move. She interrupted him several times, giving him instructions and telling him he was doing something wrong. Afterward Peggy gave her view: "I was just trying to be helpful. All I said to him was, 'You always chop the onions the wrong way,' and he got all pouty and went out for a walk without saying a word. I wound up cooking the rest of the dinner and feeling really annoyed."

From his point of view, Greg felt attacked. "When she comes after me yapping like that, she might as well be physically hitting me," he explained. Because men are so vulnerable to feeling flooded, a wife's criticism can easily cause the husband to withdraw. The wife is then likely to interpret his response as a rejection of her because she doesn't realize that he's feeling flooded—she couldn't imagine needing to withdraw over such a minor criticism, even if she were a bit hurt by it. Not understanding the intensity of what her husband is feeling, his reaction seems utterly unreasonable to her.

Many couples fall into the demand/withdraw cycle in which the wife demands more emotional confrontation, causing the husband to withdraw even more, which escalates the wife's demands. For example, Diana was talking with Bill about her feelings and thoughts on how they might improve the communication within their marriage. Instead of responding to his wife's feelings, or saying how *he* felt about it, Bill's responses tended to minimize any emotionality and rarely even touched on the issues she presented. She kept trying to get him to respond:

DIANA: We don't sit down and discuss anything unless one of us gets really mad. You know, a lot of families have what they call a weekly meeting . . . when they just sit around and talk about everything that's been going on all week, things they like and things they don't like.

BILL: We used to have those at home. [He doesn't respond to her concern that they don't communicate enough. Nor does he say how he feels about them having a weekly meeting or a time when they can communicate. This is a more subtle form of stonewalling than sitting silently, but the effects are very much the same.]

DIANA: You know if you think about it, a family or a *home* should be run like a business in that sense. You have weekly staff meetings so that everybody communicates and knows what's going on.

BILL: You want to know what the major problem is that we have at work? [Again, his responses don't address the problem of their communication, or whether he thinks a weekly meeting might be a good idea for them. He isn't giving her any feedback.]

DIANA: How many times have I asked you what's wrong and you say nothing and then a month or a week later you say what was wrong, when I probably couldn't have guessed it in a million years.

BILL: I don't know why that is, you can ask almost anybody at work what's bothering them or what's troubling them and uhhh . . . It's always communication. That's the big issue. [Again he is responding by talking about something less "hot" than the issue of communication in their marriage.]

DIANA: You know, I seriously sometimes think that as long as we've been married you just don't know that much about me at all.

BILL: Nah, I think that's true about both of us . . . maybe.

DIANA: But I'll ask you if something's wrong and you get mad because I ask you.

BILL: Well, it's hard to uhh (*pause*), it's hard to uhh, you know (*pause*), it's hard to pinpoint something for an example to answer back. [By now Bill's squirming. This conversation is starting to make him very uncomfortable, as indicated by the repetitions and pauses. He is basically telling his wife, "I can't respond to you."]

Such interactions can produce a vicious cycle, especially in marriages with high levels of conflict. The more wives complain and criticize, the more husbands withdraw and stonewall; the more husbands withdraw and stonewall, the more wives complain and criticize. This cycle must be broken if conflict-engaging marriages are to avoid dissolution.

A *wife, upon noticing that her husband is withdrawing during a tense conversation, often feels that she must raise the intensity of the interaction to keep him responsive.* She may think, "Hmmmm, I'm not really getting his attention. Maybe if I show him how angry I *really* am, he'll see that this issue is really important to me." Unfortunately, if the wife becomes belligerent and contemptuous, the husband is likely to withdraw even more from the conversation because he feels even more flooded.

One couple from my study of newlyweds provides a good example of this kind of interaction. In the following conversation, Jenny misreads or is unappreciative of Mike's calmer approach, feeling that he never listens to what she has to say. Mike has a hard time responding to her concerns and, in her opinion, takes her too lightly. She begins to use a belligerent and mocking style, seemingly in an attempt to get some kind of a reaction from him:

MIKE: Now you're saying what?

JENNY: I'm saying you don't ever listen to me when I talk to you. I can tell you four or five . . . five million times to pick up the dishes or to even do the dishes. I don't care if you do the dishes and leave me the pots, but you don't even bother to do the dishes when I ask you to . . . or like with Dad this weekend. I handed you the phone but I had no clue what was going on. I had no idea if Dad was even coming to town.

MIKE: So what's the problem?

JENNY: Gee. You aren't even listening. You aren't comprehending. You aren't saying anything one way or another, "Yes I heard you. No I didn't. Yes that sounds like a good idea. No that doesn't," because you aren't listening well enough to even know if it's an idea at all or if it's just something I'm bringing up to see if you're paying attention. [Jenny's getting red in the face. It's obvious that she's very upset, frustrated by her husband's continued nonresponsiveness.]

When a wife gets completely engulfed in emotion she will often start "kitchen-sinking"—bringing up all sorts of past and present complaints and mixing them with sarcasm and contempt. This tactic, of course, overloads the husband, causing further withdrawal. Here's another excerpt from Mike and Jenny, a little later in their argument:

JENNY: (*She sighs heavily*) You never give me a straight answer to anything.

MIKE: There wasn't a question. You just made a comment. How am I supposed to answer a comment? I can get all upset and mad, but it's pretty pointless to do that.

JENNY: You think anything is pretty pointless. You think making dinner is pointless. You think talking about what we did during the day is pointless. [She has escalated to negative mind reading, belligerence, and kitchen-sinking.]

MIKE: When we do the same thing we've done every single day for the last year it is. [He is completely avoiding her issue. Instead he's discussing the words she used in the conversation and avoiding the more painful topic of their lack of communication.]

JENNY: (*Her face is red; again she's about to cry*) At least it's talking about something and not just sitting there watching the stupid TV all night long. That's all you do anymore. (*She continues to kitchen-sink*) You come home and the first thing you do is flop on the couch and you don't say, "How was your day? Did you have any exciting customers today?" No! (*mocking husband*) "Oh, you're home. Okay, that's nice." And you go back to watching TV.

Jenny's final response is full of mockery and criticism—responses she must learn to avoid if she wants to keep her husband from withdrawing completely from their discussions.

MARITAL HOTSPOTS: SEX AND HOUSEWORK

Although gender differences can lead to a wealth of marital troubles, two conflicts occur so frequently they merit special mention: how frequently the couple has sex and who does more housework. Although these are just two among countless issues that can lead to marital flare-ups, they are so important when it comes to differences between the sexes—and both men and women need insights into the other's view—that I feel compelled to give some advice.

Men usually do want more sex than women. Because boys and girls are socialized in such different ways throughout childhood, each gender receives almost opposite messages about lovemaking. Boys learn to see sex either as pure pleasure disconnected from emotional commitment, or as a vehicle for getting close to a girl. For many teenage boys and men, there are no emotional prerequisites for having sex because closeness is the goal, not the cause, of a sex act.

In contrast, women by and large need to feel physical and emotional closeness and tenderness before wanting to have sex. Making love *confirms* intimacy rather than creates it for most women. I can't count how often I've heard women complain, "He never touches me or says sweet things unless he wants sex, and I need affection on a daily basis in order to feel sexy." Or, "He goes straight for my erogenous zones. I don't want him to touch my breasts or my clitoris first thing. Even though I've told him this, he never remembers that I like to be caressed all over, hugged, kissed, massaged, and cherished first. Otherwise, sex doesn't feel good. It feels invasive." Another common sexual turnoff for women is that men want to have sex even if they are feeling distant, argumentative, or angry. Such differences can make women pull away from sexual expression in their marriages, leading to serious marital trouble.

What can be done about this problem? The major advice here is for men. Learn to empathize with your wife's prerequisites for sexual intimacy. Of course, every woman is different and you must learn, remember, and use what you discover about your wife's preferences. In general, though, a wife will probably feel sexually closer to you if at other times you tend to be physically affectionate, considerate, attentive, interested, and respectful toward her. The same is true for lovemaking itself. Learn to take time to enjoy the type of pleasuring that your wife prefers and needs. As for women, you must also understand these gender differences in sexual enjoyment and accommodate your husband's needs and preferences some of the time.

Housework may seem like a trivial concern compared to sexuality, but women see it as a major issue affecting their sex life, as well as the overall quality of their marriage. I've interviewed newlywed men who told me with pride, "I'm not going to wash the dishes, no way. That's a woman's job." Two years later, the same guys asked me, "Why don't my wife and I have sex anymore?" They just don't understand how demeaning their attitude about housework is toward their wives. Treating your wife as a servant will almost inevitably affect the more intimate, fragile parts of a relationship. Being the sole person in a marriage to clean the toilet is definitely not an aphrodisiac!

If you are a husband who is now saying, "Not me. I do my fair share," you need to take a really good look at how much you actually do around the house. Men are just not reliable reporters of how much housework and child care they do—almost every man overestimates the time he puts in. Out of a group of fifty self-described "liberated" men who stated that their wives' careers were just as important as their own, not one had ever initiated a discussion with his wife about how to divide up household tasks. Even in dual-career families, women nearly always wind up doing most of the housework. One study showed that men who claim to support feminist ideas only do an average of *four minutes* more housework each day than traditional men with openly "macho" belief systems. That adds up to scrubbing one pot or vacuuming one rug.

The message you send your wife when you do so little around the house is a lack of respect for her. Consider this conversation between

Lawrence, who does not care about keeping the house cleaner, and Marsha, who thinks housework should be a joint effort—and that she's already doing her share. He seems blind to the connection between how little housecleaning he does and how she feels about him:

MARSHA: I don't want to live in a messy house. . . . You can't look at our house as *my* house that you *help* with.

LAWRENCE: Do you feel bad about me not doing the housework up to your standards?

MARSHA: Yes, I do.

LAWRENCE: Then why don't you just do it all yourself?

MARSHA: I can't just do it all. You don't understand that, do you? You never understood that. You never will.

LAWRENCE: No, I don't. I have no intention of spending my life puttering around the house.

MARSHA: If you have no intention of doing half the work, who is going to do it? Who do you expect to do it?

LAWRENCE: (*Coughs*) Beats me.

MARSHA: Want to try again?

LAWRENCE: Yeah. A maid . . .

MARSHA: Until we can afford a maid, I don't want you to help me in "my chores" because I'm telling you that the role of woman is . . .

LAWRENCE: I don't give a damn about your role . . .

MARSHA: When you're cleaning, who are you helping?

LAWRENCE: I'm helping you.

MARSHA: No. You're helping *us*.

LAWRENCE: Us?

MARSHA: We're two people living together. We're an "Us."

Later Marsha told me that she had "given up" trying to get Lawrence to do his share. Sadly, Marsha is not alone. Even well-educated, competent, self-confident women so accept their roles as "good wives" and "good moms" that they are often reluctant to ask their spouses for more help. Although they feel exploited, they would rather just do the housework themselves than argue endlessly about it.

Of course, there are many men who do help. But sometimes there are more subtle dimensions to housework and child-care inequity. Virginia, a happily married woman, mother of three, and full-time schoolteacher, told me that she and her friends were constantly joking about their spouses. "We think of our husbands—many of whom are well-respected professors, artists, scientists, and community leaders—as being just another one of the kids in our families," she laughs. "In my case, my husband's better than most of the men I know—he cleans, he shops, he takes care of the kids. But what really drives me up a wall is that he's always asking me, 'Where's the mayonnaise?' Or, 'What do we need at the store?' Sometimes, I want to yell at him, 'Figure it out yourself. You can count onions as well as I can,' but I know I shouldn't get so annoyed," she says with an exasperated sigh. Old attitudes die hard!

So what's the solution? Psychologists Claire Rabin and Pepper Schwartz have found that when wives and husbands make what they both feel is a successful effort to divide chores fairly, both spouses benefit. Inequities in housework and child care have profound consequences for the marital satisfaction of women, which has to affect the quality of the marriage for the man as well.

Simply put, men can short circuit this hot marital issue by accepting that housework and child care are not a woman's exclusive domain. They are a couple's job. If you are a husband, you are not doing your wife a favor by "helping" with the housework—you are sharing in necessary chores to make your lives more comfortable. Try viewing housework as a good workout. Beware of hidden feelings that make the garbage seem heavier than it really is, or the pile of dishes seem higher than it really is. And remember: men who do more housework and child care have better sex lives and happier marriages than others.

Doing housework may also be good for a man's health. This may sound far-fetched, but we found a direct correlation between how much housework a man does and the likelihood that he'll be physically more healthy four years later! Perhaps resolving this major marital issue means there is less conflict at home, so the man experiences less stress over the years.

Many women who are otherwise assertive are reluctant to confront their husbands about these issues, particularly when it comes to child care. Perhaps they feel too guilty to ask for more help, thinking that child care ought to be primarily their role. Men would be well advised to be vigilant for inequities in child care and housework, and to ask their wives if there is a problem—women are unlikely to bring it up until their mounting frustration leads to an explosion. And men will get many points for their thoughtfulness.

ADVICE FOR HIM AND HER

Men and women are different in the way they will be tracked through various parts of the diagnosis of an ailing marriage. Let me summarize these differences.

PREFERRED STYLE OF RESOLVING CONFLICT

Wives are often the caretakers of intimacy in marriages, so they wind up being the ones to bring up issues. Women have better memories for social events than men, and are better at not getting so upset and disorganized by strong negative emotions. Men are more likely to want to avoid conflict when the negative emotions get intense. They try to be rational, conciliatory, and tend to rush too quickly toward a rational attempt to "solve" the problem (usually meaning to make it go away) before really understanding and empathizing with their wife's feelings.

The Four Horsemen. Husbands are the great stonewallers. But wives are more likely to criticize, which can cause flooding in their husbands (it takes outright contempt to start flooding in most women). Flooding, in turn, leads husbands to stonewall.

Distress-Maintaining Thoughts. Men are more likely to nourish these kinds of thoughts than women, which may explain why men take longer to recover from physiological arousal than women. Women are better at self-soothing than men.

Marital History. I was surprised to find that the husband's memories are crucial here. In the interview about the history of the marriage (how they met, the wedding, and so on) the husband's fondness for his wife, the husband's sense of we-ness, the husband's being expansive (talking a lot about how they met, what first attracted him to her), and the husband's disappointments with the marriage were far more predictive of whether the couple would stay together than were the wife's responses. Husbands can help simply by making a greater effort to change the negatives to positives in thinking back over the course of the marriage, recalling more about the good times.

In the next chapters, I'll go into detail about the steps both of you can take to make your conflicts constructive rather than destructive no matter how far off the track you think you've come. But just as there are two marriages, his and hers, certain advice applies more to men than women and vice versa. So keep in mind the following general suggestions as you read the rest of the book:

ADVICE FOR MEN: EMBRACE HER ANGER

The most important advice I can give to men who want their marriages to work is to try *not* to avoid conflict. Sidestepping a problem won't make it go away—on the contrary, leaving the conflict unresolved will just upset your wife more. Realize that she needs to talk about what's eating at her to keep the relationship working smoothly. Unpleasant though it may be for you, by venting her feelings she is working to keep your marriage healthy. Try to remember that her goal is not to attack you personally, even though it may seem so at times if frustration causes her to couch her complaints in contempt and sarcasm. If you stay with her through this discomfort and listen to her criticisms rather than insisting that she's exaggerating or getting hysterical over nothing, she will calm down. If you stonewall and refuse to listen, she'll be edgy and may escalate the conflict, making it more likely that you'll wind up feeling flooded.

For example, your wife tells you how to load the dishwasher, saying, "I've told you a hundred times to put the glasses on the top.

If you do it the other way, they won't get clean." You may be thinking, "What difference does it make where I put the darned glasses? Who cares if they have a few streaks on them—we're not entertaining the president." So you may try to end the conversation, to leave, or to contradict her.

Instead, try saying something soothing to yourself like, "It may not be important to me, but obviously, it's important to her so I'll listen. Her anger is her way of underlining how important this is to her. She is just trying to make sure she has my attention." And after listening to her complaint, why not agree to do it better if it pleases her? Or, in a friendly, humorous way, you could offer to conduct a scientific experiment to see which glasses get cleaner—the ones on top or the ones on bottom. After all, it isn't really the cleanliness of the glasses that is most important to your wife; it's the *validation of her feelings* by you that really counts.

This doesn't mean that you have to "give in" to all of your wife's criticisms. But you should always respect her opinion and try to understand what she's saying rather than reacting like you're on automatic pilot. In every situation, you have a choice about how to respond to your wife's demands. By becoming more aware of your tendency to get defensive whenever your wife criticizes you, you can learn to short circuit this negative reaction. In this way, a disagreement can last for a minute or two, instead of the usual hour or more.

Above all, remember that your wife really cares about your relationship. That's why she keeps confronting you. She wants the two of you to resolve your problems together. If you want your marriage to work, you have to be willing to take your wife as she comes— including what may seem like her trivial criticisms of you.

ADVICE FOR WOMEN: CONFRONT HIM GENTLY

To break out of the vicious cycle of demand/withdrawal, you need to realize that you and your husband are emotionally from different planets. In our culture, women still bear the major responsibility for raising issues in a marriage. But you need to try to do so in a calm and gentle manner; otherwise your husband is likely to withdraw. Don't take it personally if he tries to prematurely derail an important conversation by, for example, changing the subject. It's important to make him face up to conflicts between you, but let him know you are not attacking him. Instead of saying, "You never load the dishwasher," try saying something like, "I feel upset when you don't load the dishwasher." Or: "This may not seem important to you, but it is to me—and so we need to talk about it."

When you do criticize your husband, remember to tell him you still love him and that you just want him to change a certain behavior. Try very hard not to slip from complaint to criticism and then to contempt. He will easily get flooded and then the conflict can quickly escalate. It will be much easier for him to stay engaged if you let him know that talking together about what's bothering you is a way to keep the love between you alive.

You see, women are, in general, better than men at handling hot things. My wife can empty a steaming hot pot of spaghetti with her bare hands. With the same pot, I have to use lots of hot pads. I'd burn my hands if I tried picking it up her way. And it's not much different with emotions.

FOR BOTH: ACCEPTANCE

Finally, the best advice I can give both of you is to accept your differences. For biological and cultural reasons, you can't ever expect the opposite sex to completely understand who you are and what you want. There really are two marriages: his and hers. But by appreciating and respecting your basic dissimilarities these two marriages can coexist in a supportive, harmonious union.

SIX

YOUR MARRIAGE:
THE DIAGNOSIS

By now you have taken tests that analyze your marriage in several key areas. Seeing clearly where the fault lines and shaky points are in your relationship is the first step in making your marriage stronger. Just as the results from a blood test give you a profile of what's healthy and what needs attention, so do these tests of your marriage. In the following chapters I'll suggest remedies—some very specific to these diagnoses, others general enough that most every couple will benefit from them.

YOUR MARRIAGE: A DIAGNOSTIC CHECKLIST

Summarize the diagnosis of your marriage by checking any of the areas in which there is a problem.

Marital Style (test on page 51): Do differences exist between you and your partner in what style of conflict resolution to have—Avoider? Validator? Volatile?
YOU: Yes   No   YOUR PARTNER: Yes   No

Love and Respect (test on page 63): Is there enough in your marriage?

You: Yes   No   YOUR PARTNER: Yes   No

The Four Horsemen: Do you or your partner have problems with any of the four horsemen:

Criticism? (test on page 77)

You: Yes   No   YOUR PARTNER: Yes   No

Contempt? (test on page 81)

You: Yes   No   YOUR PARTNER: Yes   No

Defensiveness? (test on page 90)

You: Yes   No   YOUR PARTNER: Yes   No

Stonewalling? (test on page 96)

You: Yes   No   YOUR PARTNER: Yes   No

Distress-maintaining Thoughts (test on page 108): Is the "innocent-victim" pattern characteristic of your thoughts?

      Yes   No

Is the "righteous indignation" pattern characteristic of your thoughts? (test on page 108)

You: Yes   No   YOUR PARTNER: Yes   No

The Distance and Isolation Cascade: Where do you stand on the distance and isolation cascade? Flooded? (test on page 114)

      Yes   No

Do you think your marital problems are severe? (test on page 121)

      Yes   No

Do you think it isn't worth talking things over with your partner? (test on page 122)

      Yes   No

Have you already arranged your lives in parallel? (test on page 124)

      Yes   No

Are you lonely in your marriage? (test on page 125)

      Yes   No

Your marital history (test on page 132): What do you tell yourself about the history of your marriage?

Are you feeling more negative than positive about your marriage?
YOU: Yes   No   YOUR PARTNER: Yes   No

DIAGNOSES AND THEIR REMEDIES

Let's take these diagnoses—and where you can find help with their remedies—one by one.

MARITAL STYLE

If there are no major differences between you and your partner over what style of conflict resolution to have, this stability should make your marriage less vulnerable to the four horsemen. But even if you've arrived at a stable style, you may still find that there are specific problem areas which, if you let them go unchecked, could start to destabilize your marriage.

If there are large differences in the kind of marriage you and your spouse prefer, then you are easier prey for the forces that can destabilize a relationship. In many unstable marriages there was never any agreement about what type of marriage to have. For example, a person who would be happy in a volatile marriage may have inadvertently married a conflict avoider, and both of them have tried in vain to accommodate the other's preferences.

Look at your answers to the test in chapter 2, on page 51. If you said that you both were conflict avoiders you don't have a problem with this area of your marriage. If you said that you were both conflict engagers, go on to the diagnosis based on the second part of this test.

Did you answer the first part as follows?

1. *You: Conflict Avoider; Spouse: Conflict Engager.* If you feel most comfortable with a conflict avoider style but your spouse is a conflict engager, you probably feel overwhelmed by your spouse's combativeness and feel that your partner keeps demanding things of you that you cannot provide.

2. *You: Conflict Engager; Spouse: Conflict Avoider.* If you feel most comfortable with a conflict engager style but your spouse is a conflict avoider, your partner probably feels that you always bring

conflict into the marriage, that it is your problem, that you are overly emotional and too demanding. You feel frustrated that you can't really talk to your partner about your feelings. The marriage seems too distant and unemotional to you and you are frustrated that problems don't seem to get resolved.

Now let's look at your answers to the second part. If you said that you were both volatile, or if you said that you were both validators, you do not have a problem with this area of the marriage. But did you answer as follows?

1. *You: Validator; Partner: Volatile.* You probably find your partner overly argumentative and provocative, even belligerent at times. You feel that you hardly get a chance to express your feelings before your partner is trying to convince you that your very feelings are wrong. You don't feel that your partner listens to you very well. You also may find your partner quite controlling and domineering. At times you dislike your partner's strong need for independence and autonomy and wish that the two of you could function more smoothly as a unit, as a "we."

2. *You: Volatile; Your Partner: Validator.* You get annoyed by your partner's emotional detachment and seeming unflappability. Sometimes you'd do anything to get a rise or any response out of your partner. You feel that your needs for separateness and autonomy are not understood. At times you feel smothered and need psychological space. You want your partner to see you as a separate individual, not part of a marriage. You wish that your partner were a more emotional person and also at times wish that your partner enjoyed a good argument or debate more. Your discussions are a bit too bland for your taste.

Remedy. Even couples who have found agreement on the marital type they want can use some help ensuring that the four horsemen stay far from their door. Remember that it takes some effort to protect even the happiest marriage from starting to slide down the marital rapids. The key is managing your disagreements well. Advice for validating couples is on page 204, for volatile couples on page 205, and for conflict-avoiding couples on page 209.

Mismatches in marital style open the way for the four horsemen and other patterns of reactivity that can destabilize a marriage. If there are mismatches between you and your partner on your preferred marital style, you will benefit by focusing on the particular symptoms that signify your marriage is in danger of losing its stability. Tackle each of the specific problems that have been diagnosed by the following tests, and put your efforts into mastering the remedies and antidotes for these problems that are detailed in the chapters that follow. It will also help for you and your spouse to read the recommendations for handling disagreements specific to each marital style (pages 214–22), and to talk over which feel most comfortable to you to see if you can come to a mutual understanding about how to treat complaints and grievances between you.

"THE FOUR HORSEMEN OF THE APOCALYPSE"

Do you or your partner have problems with any of the four horsemen?

CRITICISM (test on page 77).
If either you or your partner came out high on criticism, you have a common problem. If your partner is high on criticism but you are not, you probably often feel unfairly attacked. If you score high but your partner does not, you probably feel you need to be critical because it is so hard to bring about change in your partner. You are frustrated with the continual lack of resolution of issues, and may resent being turned into a nag by your partner. If you are both high on criticism you have fallen into a pattern that will eventually be destructive to your marriage. When you are criticized you can easily feel that there is something wrong with you, and are likely to feel hurt and unappreciated. And it is hard to respond positively to a criticism, since it is an attack on your personality: if you agree, you are joining in the attack on your self; if you disagree, you appear defensive. It is very hard to respond constructively to a Criticism.

Remedy. The antidote to being too critical is learning to state your grievances and complaints in a manner that your spouse will not take as a personal attack. You need to learn to make your criticisms more specific, and to state them as complaints. See page 181.

CONTEMPT *(test on page 81)* Contempt is directly corrosive of love in marriages. It would be far better if both you and your partner felt respected and rarely acted contemptuously toward one another. But if that is not the case, how can you respond? If your partner is contemptuous of you, it can make you feel somewhere between furious and worthless. It is very difficult to live with someone who insults you; contempt is a form of psychological abuse.

Remedy. Whichever partner is prone to speaking with contempt needs to replace that habit with the expression of genuine validation and admiration (see page 195). And, beyond that, your marriage needs to be nurtured by the intentional enhancement of the positive-to-negative ratio.

DEFENSIVENESS *(test on page 90)*
If you said that you are not defensive but your spouse is, you may not have been completely honest with yourself. Defensiveness is almost always a two-way street. Or perhaps you are in an unusual situation, married to a very defensive person, who becomes defensive at the drop of a hat. In either case it will help to take a hard look at the way you state your complaints and express your anger. It could be that your partner is emotionally flooded by the way you express your negative feelings about the relationship. Or, perhaps, your partner is reacting to you as if you were someone else in your partner's past who was a verbal attacker. Defensiveness is often best thought of as a form of fear or response to a perceived attack, real or imagined.

Remedy. Calming down is the first order of business. If you are defensive, then you are probably starting (or well on your way to) feeling emotionally flooded by your partner's expressions of negativity. In this case you need to be able to soothe yourself; see methods for calming down on page 176. You also have to take a hard look at any distress-maintaining thoughts you have; see page 179 for strategies for changing these mental habits. And you can attack the problem directly by mastering ways to speak and listen nondefensively (see page 181).

Stonewalling (test on page 96)

When someone is stonewalling you, you are likely to feel judged, or that your partner is disapproving, detached, cold, smug, or superior. You feel that your partner doesn't respond to you, doesn't care about your feelings. It is as if your partner walked out on you, abandoning you, even if physically present.

On the other hand, stonewallers usually think they are being "neutral," not negative. The stonewaller wants to disengage, calm down, maybe even run away. The stonewaller is overwhelmed by all this negative emotion and wants to withdraw without making things worse. The stonewaller may be trying to calm down and may even be thinking positive thoughts about the partner, like "I love her even though I'm upset now; I shouldn't take all this too personally. Just calm down." Or the stonewaller may be feeling hurt, wanting to either leave for a time or to get even.

What about marriages where there are two stonewallers? Such couples are on the way toward a hostile-detached marriage, one of the two styles most likely to break up.

Remedy. Like people who are defensive, you need to master ways to calm down (see page 176), to listen and speak nondefensively (page 181), and to change your distress-maintaining thoughts to more helpful ones (page 179).

OTHER PROBLEMS

Cycle of Negativity (no test, but described on pages 97–98)

Do you have access to normal repair mechanisms? Is the ratio of positive to negative at least 5 to 1? The signs of trouble are long cycles of negative response, in which one negative is met with a counter-negative. There seems to be no way out of this trap. All interaction goes awry.

Remedy. The antidotes to this cycle are repair mechanisms (see page 219). These operate in most strong relationships, even though they are usually said with negative emotional tone. For example, "Stop interrupting me!" is typically said with some irritation. But in satisfying marriages these repair tactics work.

You also need to recalibrate the positive-to-negative ratio, so that positives predominate. This requires that you purposely engage in a very rich schedule of positive events and moments.

DISTRESS-MAINTAINING THOUGHTS (test on page 108)

When distressing thoughts about your partner and the relationship become cast in stone, it can be very destructive to your marriage. Is the innocent victim or the righteous indignation pattern characteristic of your thoughts? If so, you are setting yourself up to feel emotionally flooded. And what you think, even if it is known only to yourself, has a great deal of impact on how you treat your partner.

Remedy. You first need to become aware of these thought patterns, catching them as they take you over. Then you need to realize that you don't have to believe these thoughts—you can change them instead (see page 179).

THE DISTANCE AND ISOLATION CASCADE (test on page 121)

If you are feeling flooded (test on page 114), then you will probably begin to avoid your partner, perhaps without even realizing you are doing it. If you think your marital problems are severe, then you may have begun losing hope. If you think it isn't worth talking things over with your partner, you are moving toward despair about ever being able to resolve the conflict in your marriage, a sign that you are emotionally divorcing your partner. Have you already arranged your lives in parallel? Often the process of parallel lives is imperceptible, but it is one of the final stages before a breakup. Are you lonely in your marriage? The possibility of easing your pain with someone else increases as you become lonely; extramarital affairs occur for all kinds of reasons, but loneliness is one of the most common.

Remedy. The pivotal pressure that is the keystone to this cascade of distance and isolation is from feeling flooded. If you can learn to calm these feelings of being emotionally overwhelmed by your partner, it opens the way for other ways to repair your marriage. To relieve the sense of being flooded, you need to calm down (page 176); to change distress-maintaining thoughts (page 179); and to speak and listen non-defensively (page 181).

NEGATIVE MARITAL HISTORY (test on page 132)

What do you and your partner tell yourselves about your past together? This is a sign of trouble if either of you are disappointed, find it hard to express fondness or admiration, can't remember what first attracted you, find little in common, and have trouble valuing the struggles you've gone through. If this is true for you or for your partner, then there is a real danger that one or both of you has gone a final step toward being closed to your marriage. The situation may not be hopeless, but it is serious, even desperate.

Remedy. The antidotes to such a negative view of your marriage are to change your distress-maintaining thoughts (see page 179) and to better handle feelings of being flooded by learning ways to calm down (page 176).

HIS AND HERS MISUNDERSTANDINGS

The unique tendencies of men and women can feed the difficulties in your marriage. Men may be more likely than their wives to be flooded by criticism, while for women flooding does not typically occur until there is contempt. Once flooded, men usually have more trouble calming down physiologically than their wives, and stay physiologically aroused longer. Being flooded means they will not process information as well, not listen as well, and turn to escape or attack.

For men, this pattern shows up as a husband who reacts to being flooded by his wife's criticism by avoiding talking about disagreements, or by stonewalling. If this is your pattern, you may try to dismiss or deal with your wife's negative feelings too quickly, perhaps because you think they are dangerous or cloud one's judgment. Or you may avoid the feelings by diving into work or hobbies, or rush to problem solve before understanding the feelings.

For women, the gender discrepancy results in a wife who comes on too strong in airing complaints, or feels frustrated by an unresponsive husband. This can occur if, in general, you expect to understand your feelings about disagreements with people who are close to you, get support, and then to problem solve only once the feelings are understood. But you may not realize that your husband has less experience with this way of dealing with strong negative feelings, and so you may incorrectly interpret his withdrawal and avoidance as a personal rejection.

Remedy. Wives who criticize instead of complaining trigger the flooding in their husbands that leads to stonewalling. If this is happening in your marriage, master the art of complaining without criticism or contempt (see page 188). Husbands who feel overwhelmed by their wives' complaints will benefit by learning to listen nondefensively (page 185), validating their wives (page 195), and mastering ways to calm down, the antidote to being flooded (see page 181).

WHAT TO DO ABOUT YOUR MARITAL DIAGNOSIS

IF YOU HAVE TROUBLE WITH:	TRY THESE REMEDIES:
Differences in marital style	Choose a style together, see page 202.
Criticism	Learn to make more specific complaints, see page 188; validate your partner, page 196.
Contempt	Enhance the 5-to-1 ratio. Express genuine validation and admiration, see page 196.
Defensiveness or Stonewalling	Master: Calming down, see page 176. Nondefensive listening and speaking, see page 185 and page 188. Dealing with distress-maintaining thoughts, see page 179.

Distress-maintaining thoughts	Become aware of and redesign these thoughts, see page 179.
Flooding	Calming down, page 176. Dealing with distress-maintaining thoughts, page 179. Nondefensive listening and speaking, page 185 and page 188.
Distance and Isolation Cascade	Flooding is the key to truncating this cascade. See above.
Your Marital History	To avoid rewriting your marital history in negatives, you need to better handle flooding (see above) and distress-maintaining thoughts, see page 179. And try telling your story in a positive light, page 226.
His and Hers	*For Men:* Listen nondefensively, page 185. Validate your wife, page 195, and calm down. *For Women:* Complain without criticism or contempt, page 188.

SEVEN

THE FOUR KEYS TO
IMPROVING YOUR MARRIAGE

In the last chapter I asked you to summarize your marital profile in the areas where couples most often have problems. In this chapter I am going to tell you what you can do about them. Of course these problems are related, and several are consequences of others. So while some problems have specific antidotes, many respond to the same remedies.

FOUR SIMPLE THINGS YOU CAN DO

By now it's probably clear to you that I believe some conflict and disagreement are crucial for a marriage's long-term success. The idea that conflict is healthy may sound like a cruel joke if you're feeling overwhelmed by the negativity in your relationship. But in a sense a marriage lives and dies by what you might loosely call its arguments, by how well disagreements and grievances are aired. The key is *how* you argue—whether your style escalates tension or leads to a feeling of resolution.

You may assume that learning a healthy disagreement style is a complex, virtually impossible task. Far from it. Although many marriage manuals offer long lists of communication techniques you can follow, I think that most couples (even those in the most miserable marriages) don't really need an intricate, step-by-step program. After all, the same couples who are unable to communicate at home easily do so with their neighbors or at work. Sometimes a marital discussion that is going nowhere will be interrupted by a telephone call and it's amazing to see how capable a communicator the same person is with someone else. Then it's back to the identical frustrating discussion after the phone call, and back to the same old reactions that don't work in the marriage.

Obviously, the problem isn't a lack of skill. It's that their ability to communicate with their loved one is stymied by the negativity that's enveloping their marriage. It's all too easy to let simple disagreements become knock-down, drag-out fights that leave one or both of you wondering if this marriage can be saved. The real problem is a lack of strategy—in other words, losing sight of when to apply the skills you already have.

In fact, I believe there are only four crucial strategies that you need to utilize in order to break through most of the negativity. If you can put them to use, your marriage is almost certain to improve dramatically—all your natural communication and conflict-resolving abilities will come to the fore. Of course, it won't always be easy to put these essentials to work. It will take courage, strength, and trust to use them when you're feeling hurt, angry, and victimized. The key is not only to understand these strategies intellectually but to use them so often that they become second nature and are available to you *even when you are feeling very upset*—the moments you'll need them most. I call this *over-learning* and it is the one principle you need to adopt for my program to work at all.

Master these fundamentals and I think you'll be at least 75 percent of the way toward maximizing your marital happiness. Then, if you're ready for more detailed advice on communication, go on to the next chapter, where I offer an array of further techniques that you can try. Don't think you and your spouse need to use each of them systematically. Just choose the few that suit you and your needs.

Much of the advice in this chapter concerns how to approach your spouse during a discussion of disagreements or issues. I am avoiding using the word *fight* because that word may not accurately fit your interactions. Some couples, especially avoiders, sidestep scrapes but still have low-key disagreements. The same advice applies to them as well.

I may surprise you by claiming that you ought not to worry so much about solving your marital problems as in dealing with the emotions they stir. In fact, what a couple in one type of stable marriage means by "solving" the problem will be entirely different than what another means.

If problem solving isn't the main goal of my recommendations, then what is? The major goal is to break the cycle of negativity and give whatever natural repair mechanisms you already have in your repertoire a chance to work. There are four key strategies for accomplishing this goal.

In the following pages, I'll explain how to incorporate the four strategies for a lasting healthy marriage into your own relationship. The major goal is to break the cycle of negativity. You'll learn (1) how to *calm yourself* so that flooding doesn't block your communication; (2) how to *speak and listen nondefensively* so that your discussions or disagreements will be more productive; (3) how to *validate each other* as well as your relationship even (or especially) when the going gets tough; (4) how to *overlearn these principles* so that your new skills become almost second nature.

As you read on, you may feel that some of the strategies sound a bit unnatural or alien to you. Don't worry about absorbing them all in one sitting. As with any new endeavor, learning to argue effectively takes practice. I've left you plenty of opportunity to try out your new abilities. Have faith—you'll get there.

For starters, make an agreement with your partner to limit discussions of disagreements to fifteen minutes at a sitting. Set a kitchen timer. If you decide to go for longer at the end of fifteen minutes, add only another fifteen minutes.

STRATEGY #1: CALM DOWN

The first step is learning to calm down. This is a specific remedy for several problems, most related to flooding. It eases the need to be defensive and to stonewall, undercuts the physical feelings that sustain distress-maintaining thoughts, and is the antidote to flooding. And because flooding is the trigger for the Distance and Isolation Cascade, calming down is a preventive measure.

Because flooding is so destructive to a relationship, the first strategy you need to learn is to recognize when you're feeling overwhelmed and then to make a deliberate effort to calm yourself. From the data gathered in our lab we've seen how quickly discussions fall apart as soon as one spouse's heart rate begins to soar. Because physical responses are such an accurate barometer of your ability to communicate at a particular moment, tracking your arousal level during intense conversation will keep your discussions on track as well. Learning to calm down helps prevent unproductive fighting or running away from discussions you need to have. The notion of monitoring your physical responses and calming yourself are direct applications of my insights into couples during marital conflict resolution.

Calming down is the exact physiological opposite of flooding. When you're flooded, you are extremely upset and physiologically aroused. By calming down you take a direct step toward reversing that distress.

Calming down is especially important for men, since as we know, they are more likely to feel physiologically overwhelmed sooner than women during a heated marital exchange. And it takes less intense negativity for men to get physiologically overwhelmed. Also, men are more likely to rehearse destructive, innocent-victim or vengeful thoughts once they feel flooded. But whatever your gender, it's virtually impossible to think straight when your blood is pumping furiously and your heart is racing. For that reason you're likely to fall back on automatic, overlearned behavior once you become flooded. This is why overarousal leads you to say things you later regret, why you may want to run away, why you stonewall, why you may fly off the handle— and why it would be better to take a deep breath and simply soothe yourself.

For all these reasons you should take your pulse every five minutes or so during difficult discussions with your spouse as a way to monitor your physiological reactions, specifically your heart rate. You may think pulse-taking is silly and unnecessary, but most people are actually very poor judges of their own heart rates. A quick check of your pulse will ensure that you're aware of your true arousal level. Taking your pulse is fairly simple—you may already have learned to do it during aerobic exercise or to monitor a heart condition.

Gently press your right index and middle fingers against your right carotid artery, which is two-to-three inches below your earlobe and under your jawbone. You should be able to feel your pulse. To calculate your pulse rate per minute, count the number of pulse beats you feel in fifteen seconds and multiply by four. To determine your average, baseline rate, take your pulse three different times while you're sitting comfortably. Although individual pulse rates vary widely, most women clock in at between 82 and 86 beats per minute while men average between 72 and 76 beats per minute.

Once you know your baseline rate, it's simple to check your arousal level during discussions. If at any time your rate climbs to 10 percent above your resting rate (an increase of about 8 to 10 beats per minute), you know you're overaroused and need to take a break.

This chart can help you assess your pulse rate:

BASELINE HEART RATE: _____
10 PERCENT OF BASELINE: _____
SUM OF THE ABOVE: _____   (*Your heart rate*
during discussions should not
exceed this.)

If, for example, your baseline rate is 80, it's best to take a break if you hit 88. It is absolutely crucial that you take a break if your heart rate goes over 100 BPM. When your heart is beating that fast, your body is releasing relatively larger quantities of adrenaline than it normally does, triggering a panicky fight-or-flight stress reaction that will make it virtually impossible for you to absorb what your partner is saying.

At first it may feel forced and artificial to request an intermission when your spouse is sounding off about, say, your sloppy showering habits. But if you clarify why you're doing it, and both agree to use this strategy, over time you'll both get used to it. Explain that you're not trying to avoid the discussion. On the contrary, taking a break now will simply allow you to calm down so you'll be better able to hear and understand your partner's point of view.

Call a time-out using whatever method feels most comfortable to you: hold up both hands or simply announce to your mate that it's time to knock off for a bit. This is not unlike the bell that sends two fighters retreating to their corners during a bout—except that your goal when you return is to communicate better, not pummel each other.

How long do you think it will take you to calm down? Many people guess about five minutes. In fact, it takes most people closer to twenty minutes for their physiological responses to return to baseline. As I mentioned, many of us are surprisingly poor judges of our own heart rates. In fact, most people believe they have calmed down completely when their pulse rate is still a good 10 percent above their normal, resting pulse. It is easy to *think* you've settled down when actually you're still riled up. So be sure to take your pulse before returning to the discussion.

There's an important reason you should not return until you're truly calm: a psychological phenomenon called the "Zillmann Transfer of Excitation Effect." Studies show that if you believe you have calmed down but are still physiologically aroused when you reapproach your spouse, you'll be very susceptible to taking on any emotion he or she expresses. In other words, you'll channel your remaining physiological excitation toward duplicating whatever emotion is prevailing at the moment. So if your partner is still angry when you resume your talk, you'll pick up the anger as well, defeating the purpose of your time-out.

What should you do during the recess? Whatever will soothe you. For some people that means simply leaving the room. Others find it helps to hop in the car for a relaxing drive, take a bath, listen to music, cal a friend, work, and so on. But whatever your physical location, the real key to calming down is what you tell yourself.

REWRITING YOUR INNER SCRIPT

Too often, people spend a time-out rehearsing all kinds of hurtful or vengeful comments they plan to make when they return. They tend to repeat to themselves distress-maintaining thoughts—those inner scripts of righteous indignation or innocent victimization I described in chapter 4. Some typical thoughts along these lines are:

"That really hurt me."
"I can't forgive and forget what he (she) said and did."
"I will not let go of my anger and hurt."
"I'm getting out of this marriage."
"I'm not going to take this anymore."
"I'll show her (him)."
"I'll get even."
"That makes me mad."
"He (She) is *(Fill in the blank with an insult)*."
"I'm getting out of here."
"I don't deserve this."
"All the things I do, and I never get recognized or appreciated."
"I'm not going to react. I'm simply going to stand there stone-faced."

For a time-out to be effective you need to make a conscious effort to replace these distress-maintaining thoughts with soothing and validating ones. Try these:

"Calm down. Take some deep breaths."
"No need to take this personally."
"He's (she's) upset right now, but this isn't a personal attack."
"This isn't really about me."
"This is a bad moment, but things aren't always like this."
"I'm upset now, but I love him (her)."
"She (he) has a lot of nice qualities."
"There are lots of things I admire about him (her)."
"Right now I'm upset, but this is basically a good marriage."

Often when people get flooded they change their healthy patterns, holding their breath and breathing silently in shallow breaths. Some people we've interviewed found it helpful to close their eyes, breathe deeply and evenly, and pretend they were somewhere else during a time-out. If that sounds like a good strategy for you, try thoughts like:

"I'm on a beach and I can hear the waves coming in."
"I'm in a lush, green forest and I can hear the birds singing."
"It's been a long time since I played my saxophone. Maybe I should take lessons again."
"The best meal I ever had was that grilled salmon at the French restaurant we went to for our anniversary."

RELAXATION METHODS
While changing your distressing thoughts is one route to cooling off, another is to simply make yourself physically relaxed (a combination of both approaches can be especially effective). Exactly which relaxation technique will work for you is highly individual. Here are some you can experiment with:

• Sit quietly with your eyes closed and pay close attention to the sensations of your breath. As you breathe out, think to yourself, "out"; as you inhale, think, "in." Whenever your thoughts wander, bring your mind back to noticing your breath. Some people find that it is soothing to use a word with special meaning for them with each in-breath and out-breath, something like "peace," or "Jesus," for example. Try it for ten minutes or so.

• Try deep muscle relaxation, in which you systematically tense and then relax the major muscle groups throughout your body. Lie down and begin by scrunching up the muscles in your face, holding them in a state of tension, and then releasing the tension. Go slowly through your body, holding and then relaxing tension in your neck and shoulders, arms and hands, chest and stomach, pelvis, legs and feet. You should be sure to leave each set of muscles in a relaxed state as you go through the body, top to bottom.

• For some people aerobic exercise is calming. If you have an aerobic workout routine, do it for about ten minutes, until you work up a bit of a sweat. While you're working out, of course, your pulse rate will go up. But afterward there is a "rebound," so that your pulse rate is slower than before you started.

Once your pulse rate indicates that you have calmed down physically, approach your spouse and continue your discussion for another fifteen minutes.

Training yourself to take calming breaks when you're at risk of feeling flooded won't solve your marital problems. But it is an essential first step that will keep you receptive to other strategies that can help you dramatically.

STRATEGY #2: SPEAK NONDEFENSIVELY

Listening or speaking without being defensive helps counter several destructive habits. Nondefensive *listening* is especially helpful to ease defensiveness. If you are a nondefensive listener, it will make the cycle of negativity less likely. And a nondefensive attitude also helps defuse flooding and the need to stonewall, particularly for men. But defensiveness is a two-way street; if you start *speaking* nondefensively, you will lessen your partner's need to be defensive.

And if you can learn to listen and to speak with your spouse without feeling the need to defend yourself and without triggering defensiveness in your mate, you'll do wonders for your marriage. Defensiveness is one of the most dangerous of the four horsemen, and it can lead to endless spirals of negativity. By finding the courage not to be defensive (or at least recognizing and minimizing it as much as possible) your marriage will almost certainly improve.

This will be tough to do at first. After all, listening and speaking without being defensive are not strategies we learn in school, or anywhere else. But couples who work hard at weeding defensiveness out of their interactions find a dramatic rise in their marital satisfaction.

PRAISE AND ADMIRATION: UNSEATING THE FOUR HORSEMEN

The single most important tactic for short-circuiting defensive communication is to choose to have a positive mindset about your spouse and to reintroduce praise and admiration into your relationship. If your arguments are marked by defensiveness, it's likely that your marriage is being overrun by all four horsemen. As the negativity in your relationship swells, the balance of positive to negative feelings and interactions between you and your spouse is thrown off. Depending on your particular personality and circumstances, this negativity will lead you toward being mostly a critic, an abuser, or a stonewaller. But in any case, having and expressing a positive attitude toward your spouse is the most powerful antidote.

At first, this may sound Pollyannish. After all, if it were so simple to just feel good about your husband or wife, you wouldn't need to read this chapter in the first place! I'm not saying that it is so simple. But I am stating that it is certainly doable if you have a full understanding of the importance of praise and admiration and some blueprint for reintroducing them into your marriage.

Even a little bit of nondefensive listening and validation at the right times can have dramatic effects. Herb was a steady social drinker and his wife Jan complained that his drinking at his social club often left her all alone and lonely. Herb became very defensive and said that he deserved this time with his friends and that his club gave him valuable business contacts. Jan became increasingly more upset and alienated from him as the conversation progressed when suddenly, out of the blue, Herb said, "So what you'd like is if when I got to the club I called you and asked you if you wanted to come down and join me." The atmosphere changed immediately and she said, "Yes, that's it." He said, "Well, I think I can do that. Not every time, but certainly most of the time." A little while later the affection had grown so much that Jan said, "Now I know why I married you."

Even in strong relationships, too often people focus on the negatives in an effort to make the relationship all the better. But by dwelling on what is wrong in your marriage, it's easy to lose sight of what is right. This is a primary reason that admiration is often the first thing to go. Once you become aware of your spouse's negative qualities, you may forget all the attributes you long admired and valued.

To improve or save your marriage you must remind yourself that your mate's negative qualities do not cancel out all the positives that led you to fall in love. Nor do bad times wipe out all the good times. If your marriage is going through a rocky period it's particularly important to recall specific happy memories you have of your mate. Even force yourself to sit a while and think about them. For example, you could look through picture albums from past vacations, or reread some old love letters.

The bottom line is that you need to become the architect of your thoughts. It's up to you to decide what your inner script will contain. You can habitually look at what is *not* there in your relationship, at your disappointments, and fill your mind with thoughts of irritation, hurt, and contempt. Or you can do the opposite. For example, you could walk into the kitchen in the morning and fume because your partner did a lousy job of cleaning the counter and left dishes in the sink. Or you could look on the positive side—most of the dishes did get washed and you know your spouse was very tired last night. "We've been under a lot of pressure lately," you might think. "It's amazing how many things *are* getting done."

This really comes down to viewing the bottle as half full rather than half empty—the classic choice between optimism and pessimism. If you can learn to think empathetically rather than negatively about what your spouse is going through, and maintain your admiration for your spouse's good qualities, you will not be plagued with overwhelming distress-maintaining thoughts that trigger defensiveness and harm your marriage.

If looking on the bright side doesn't come naturally to you, start with small steps. Make a list of your partner's positive qualities—the things he or she does to contribute to your life together. Memorize this list and think about how much harder life would be without these positives. When you find yourself following a critical train of thought about your mate, use elements from the list to *interrupt* your thinking. Make a habit of this process and the change can be dramatic. You may want to work on restructuring your habitual thoughts together with your partner. Going through the process as a team can double the benefits.

Of course, there must be a real basis for feeling good about your partner's contributions. In so many marriages, this basis really does exist—yet it's amazing to me how easily the partners lose sight of it. You can all too readily fall into the rut of thinking critically about your marriage and what your mate is *not* doing right.

Once you begin "rethinking" your marriage, don't keep your positive thoughts to yourself. Everyone, including your spouse, responds to genuine praise, thanks, and simple heartfelt compliments on a regular basis. At first, you may need to remind yourself to speak your positive thoughts. Try to give your partner this gift every day, especially if you've been fighting a lot lately. I'm not suggesting that you lie about your feelings toward your spouse. You must be genuine. But, as I've said, if you look at your partner's actions objectively you're more than likely to find some things that are worth applauding. Here are the sorts of simple strokes that will go a long way:

> "I really appreciated your cooking dinner tonight."
> "You really handled that contractor well."
> "Thanks for calling the insurance company."
> "I just love watching you play with Jason."
> "You were a very considerate father tonight."
> "I know you've been stressed lately, and I admire the way you've been coping with it all."
> "One thing I like about you is your guts. You really stood up to her when she put you down. I admire that."
> "You were really funny tonight. I just love your sense of humor."

Don't be surprised if your spouse expresses some cynicism upon hearing your first few compliments. He or she may have become conditioned to expect negativity from you. But if you keep at it, your mate will eventually come to believe that your attitude has changed and will respond by being less defensive. Sooner or later you're likely to be on the receiving end of compliments as well.

As therapists know, it is very difficult for change to occur except in a climate of acceptance. One of the great paradoxes in therapy is that people don't change unless they feel accepted as they are. What people praise and admire tells us what they aspire to be, what they value and respect. Saying what you admire about your mate will make your partner feel accepted. Admiration is the opposite of contempt, possibly the most destructive of the horsemen. But it only works if it is genuine. It has to be real—and it can't just be empty words that are said to get an effect. Seasoning your interactions with genuine praise and admiration will significantly limit your spouse's defensiveness. But the third horseman, defensiveness, is still likely to surface in the heat of an argument. Fortunately, there are ways you can unseat him at such crucial times, whether your spouse is speaking or you are.

When You're the Listener

The key to defusing your spouse's defensiveness is to be a good listener. While your mate has the floor, it is your job to genuinely understand and empathize with the feelings behind the words you hear. I admit that this can be extremely difficult, especially if your spouse is criticizing you or yelling. The trick here is to try very hard not to take what your spouse is saying as a personal attack that demands you defend or counterattack, even if you're hearing a lot of contempt. Think of the intense negativity as simply underlining the strength of his or her feelings so that you will pay serious attention to them.

Recently a man I have never met called me for marital advice. He told me that his wife said they should consider getting a divorce and should think about what to do with the children. His question was whether he should take his wife seriously. I told him that, although I did not know his wife, I would certainly take the statement seriously. He seemed surprised by my advice, probably as surprised as I was by his question. This man had probably been ignoring many less intense signals his wife had been giving him for some time. Finally, with her ultimate escalation—with the unmistakable underlining—he took notice of her feelings.

I can't emphasize this point enough. If an issue has a history of frustrating interaction, the negative feelings will intensify over time. This is an act of both frustration and desperation. Your partner's negativity is a way of emphasizing how strongly your partner feels about the issue. Even if you strongly disagree with the words that go along with your partner's negativity, see them as a way of underlining how strongly your partner feels about the issue—a way to get you to pay attention.

Nondefensive listening doesn't mean you need to agree with your partner. Your mission is to try to understand your partner's feelings—to accept them as legitimate even if you don't share them. If you can send the message, "Gee, I don't see it that way, but I can understand why you might, given your perspective," you will have gone a long way toward repairing the damage of previous negativity. The highest level of nondefensive listening entails empathizing with your partner's emotions and viewpoint. This means putting yourself in your spouse's shoes and truly comprehending his or her feelings from within yourself.

There is a hierarchy of less powerful to very powerful nondefensive listening. Even the mildest form is effective. Just saying, "Uh-huh, go ahead, I'm listening," or "I can see why you'd feel that way," or "It makes sense that you'd feel that way," or even a periodic "Yeah," can communicate that you're trying to understand even if you don't necessarily have the same point of view. Just acknowledging that perhaps two points of view exist, and that both have some validity, is a powerful form of acceptance.

The most powerful form of nondefensive listening is to genuinely feel what your partner is feeling and communicate that empathic response. Again, this empathy has to be real for it to work. You can't pretend to be empathetic. In between these two levels are lots of variations, all of them good.

The following strategies can help improve your ability to listen nondefensively:

Embrace the Anger. Often, when people express themselves heatedly it's because they think that's the only way to make you listen. Remember that the anger or insult is really for emphasis, a "thwack" to get you to pay attention to what they're saying. If you respond defensively or stonewall to protect yourself from intense emotions, your spouse is likely to increase rather than lessen the emotional volume of his or her words. Thus, defensiveness and withdrawal will destroy any chance you have of really understanding what your partner is trying to say.

Especially for Stonewallers: Back-Channel. If you tend to stonewall, you are probably trying to defend yourself from feeling attacked by your partner's words. Obviously your withdrawal and the thoughts that accompany it make it impossible for you to be an engaged listener. Many stonewallers present blank faces to their mates, which sends the signal that they are not listening and just upsets their spouse even more. If your mate tends to complain that speaking to you is like talking to a wall, make a conscious effort not to stonewall and to send little signals that show you hear him or her. Psychologists call these signals *back channels*: they include nodding your head occasionally and making brief vocal indications that you understand, such as "uh-huh," "yeah," "oh I see," "um-hmmm." Back channels let your partner know that you haven't tuned out.

Read Facial Expressions. You can listen with your eyes as well as your ears. You'll find an amazing number of clues to what your partner is feeling by noticing more about his or her face.

Before you can read your partner accurately during an intense discussion, double-check that you really have noticed in detail what his or her face looks like in repose. Otherwise you might mistake your mate's natural resting facial features for signs of emotion. For instance, some people's mouth corners naturally turn down. This is not a sign of negative emotion unless this feature deepens or becomes otherwise amplified.

To assess your partner's facial expression, you don't have to stare intently into his or her eyes. In fact, it's usually the mouth that holds the most emotional information. In a real smile the lips turn up at the sides, eyes are crinkled, and cheeks are raised. But in a fake smile—which can mask hostility—only the mouth changes; the eyes are not involved. In an angry mouth, the lips are pressed so tightly together that they "disappear," or just the upper lip disappears.

In a contemptuous mouth the lips are together, and one corner of the mouth is pulled to the side, creating a dimple. And in a disgusted look only the upper lip is raised, either symmetrically or off to one side, or the mouth doesn't move much while the nose wrinkles up by the brow.

The eyebrows and forehead are also very expressive facial features, signaling your partner's distress. In a worried or furrowed brow, the eyebrows are pulled toward the nose, creating a vertical furrow in the forehead. In a sad brow, the eyebrows are raised in the middle, like inverted "v's." The grieving brow is like the sad brow, but the inner corners of the brows also pull together.

Beware of Your Own Body Language. Although it isn't necessary to agree with what your partner is saying, you shouldn't show signs of disapproval while listening. Avoid at all costs facial expressions that convey mockery or contempt. Don't roll your eyes, purse your lips, or twist them in a sarcastic smile.

There are two other facial expressions that send very strong signals that you're not empathizing at all with your mate. The *domineering listener* look suggests that you're ready to squelch your partner if he or she expresses anything you disagree with. In this stance your head is tilted downward and your frowning eyes are staring straight into your spouse's as if you're trying to control what your spouse is thinking.

A *belligerent* facial expression is equally counterproductive when you're attempting to listen. It is an attempt to provoke your partner. In this stance, you cock your head so that the plane of your face is turned away from your mate and you are leading with your chin. This suggests that you are just itching for a fight. Your arms may be folded across your chest, a further sign that you're blocking any information your partner is sending.

Obviously, these expressions are likely to anger or intimidate your spouse. Either way, they stymie communication. To be a good listener, make sure your facial expression and body language show that you're receptive to what your partner is saying. This will let him or her know that you really are listening and trying hard to understand. Say your wife tells you that the bank officer called threatening to foreclose on the mortgage because she has forgotten to make the payments for the last four months. Instead of erupting in anger, becoming belligerent or domineering, listen to her and imagine how badly you would feel if you were in her shoes—having to give this bad news. Let your understanding show on your face. The more you can show your comprehension by mirroring your partner's feelings through your facial expression—looking sad when he or she is, for example—the more confident your mate will be that you are really listening.

When You're the Speaker

There are times in any relationship when you don't like something your partner has just said. If your marriage has become filled with negativity, your knee-jerk response may be to express your displeasure by criticizing or expressing contempt toward your mate. Unfortunately, this is likely to make your spouse defensive, which just escalates the conflict. Your goal should be to simply *complain* to your spouse rather than make the attack personal. This is particularly crucial if you had a high score on the test for criticism or contempt.

Before you utter a word, remember that you really do have a choice. Think of your next statement as a fork in the road of your argument. Here is where you decide whether to keep the conversation reasonable by expressing a specific complaint or to head into rocky terrain by criticizing or verbalizing contempt. (If, despite good intentions, you slip and take the rocky road, you can always start over by calling a break.)

Let me clarify once more the distinctions between a complaint, a criticism, and contempt.

- A complaint is *specific*, limited to one situation. It states how you feel. ("I am upset because you didn't take out the garbage tonight.")
- A criticism tends to be global and *includes blaming* your partner. You'll often find the word *always* or *never* in a criticism. ("You never take out the garbage. Now it's overflowed and that's your fault. I can't ever rely on you.")
- Contempt adds insult to the criticism. It is verbal character assassination in which you accuse your spouse of stupidity, incompetence, etc. ("You idiot, why can't you ever remember to take out the garbage?")

———————— • ————————

COMPLAINT, CRITICISM, OR CONTEMPT?

To review once again the all-important difference between complaints, criticism, and contempt, take this quick quiz. For each statement, circle whether you think it is a sign of complaint, criticism, or contempt.

1. I am upset that you didn't pay the gas bill.
    Complaint   Criticism   Contempt
2. How can I ever trust you?
    Complaint   Criticism   Contempt
3. You are totally irresponsible.
    Complaint   Criticism   Contempt
4. You stupid jerk!
    Complaint   Criticism   Contempt
5. I should have known you'd pull something like that.
    Complaint   Criticism   Contempt

6. You are just terrible with the kids.
   Complaint   Criticism   Contempt
7. When we don't go out together I feel like you take me for granted.
   Complaint   Criticism   Contempt
8. I wish that you'd touch me more and be more affectionate.
   Complaint   Criticism   Contempt
9. Don't interrupt!
   Complaint   Criticism   Contempt
10. You just never care about my feelings.
    Complaint   Criticism   Contempt
11. Leave it to you and you screw up the vacation plans!
    Complaint   Criticism   Contempt
12. Whose fault is it then?
    Complaint   Criticism   Contempt
13. Don't tell me you didn't know any better.
    Complaint   Criticism   Contempt
14. I'm sick to death of your behavior.
    Complaint   Criticism   Contempt
15. Have you got an attitude problem?
    Complaint   Criticism   Contempt
16. When you don't listen to me I feel unimportant
    Complaint   Criticism   Contempt
17. I'm upset you didn't clean up the dishes last night.
    Complaint   Criticism   Contempt
18. You're just like your mother!
    Complaint   Criticism   Contempt
19. How can you hurt me like this?
    Complaint   Criticism   Contempt

ANSWER KEY:

1. Complaint
2. Criticism
3. Contempt
4. Contempt
5. Contempt
6. Criticism
7. Complaint
8. Complaint
9. Complaint
10. Criticism

11. Contempt
12. Criticism
13. Criticism
14. Criticism
15. Criticism
16. Complaint
17. Complaint
18. Contempt
19. Criticism

Give yourself one point for each correct answer. If you score below 16 points you may want to reread chapter 3 to get a clearer fix on the differences between the "Three C's."

———— • ————

If you understand how a complaint differs from criticism or contempt but still have difficulty controlling yourself from being negative during an argument, keep the following general guidelines in mind:

- Remove the blame from your comments.
- Say how *you* feel.
- Don't criticize your partner's personality.
- Don't insult, mock, or use sarcasm.
- Be direct.
- Stick with one situation.
- Don't try to analyze your partner's personality.
- Don't mind-read.

Most of all, try to be as specific as possible when you complain. The more concrete your grievance, the more you'll improve your partner's understanding of why you're upset. Think of your complaint as a set of directions. We all know how easy it is to follow instructions that are clear and explicit. If someone says, "Go two miles and turn right at the gas station with the big plastic dinosaur on top," you know exactly where to go. But if the same person were to simply wave his arms to the right, look to the left, and say soothingly, "It's just down there a piece. Can't miss it," you'd be headed for nowhere. In much the same way, a specific complaint lets your partner know exactly where you are, while vague complaints can be misinterpreted and get you off track.

A good way to keep a complaint specific is to couch it in what I call an "X, Y, Z" statement. Think of this approach as a kind of game in which you fill in the blanks with your particular gripe in mind: "When you did (or didn't do) X in situation Y, I felt Z."

Example: "When you didn't call to tell me you were going to be late (X) for our dinner appointment (Y), I felt frustrated (Z)." Using this X, Y, Z formula will help you avoid insults and character assassination. It allows you to simply state how your partner's behavior affects your feelings and, in turn, your response.

Let's say you're upset about the family finances. It's more constructive to say, "When you bounced several checks (X) and the bank called (Y), I felt embarrassed and angry (Z)," rather than, "You are incredibly irresponsible for bouncing a check. I'm constantly having to pick up after your mistakes and fix everything you screw up."

Another example of a specific complaint: "I felt so left out when you spent all night at your sister's house." (You can change the order of the X, Y, and Z to fit the way you naturally talk.) This is far more helpful to your partner than saying, "You're never home at night, I don't even feel married to you anymore." Although the latter may be what first comes to your mind, it's really just an exercise in verbal fog—and it's likely to draw a defensive response from your spouse.

It's especially common for couples to be nonspecific when talking about sexual issues, a discussion that is by its nature delicate and sensitive and therefore prone to defensiveness: "I'm just not very satisfied with sex" or "You could be a better lover" is pretty devastating news and pretty perplexing since it leaves your partner not knowing where or how to respond—except with hurt feelings.

Compare that with, "When you touch me here before we've cuddled for a while it's hard for me to relax," or, "When you want to have sex right when I get home from work it makes me feel dehumanized." (Incidentally, sex talks go even better if you emphasize what you *do* enjoy rather than what you don't: "I really like it when you touch me here," "It's so much fun when we make time to take a bath together," etc.)

Two other manners of speaking that can trigger a defensive response in your spouse are a belligerent and domineering style. Domineering speech lets your spouse know you want him or her to respond only as you see fit. ("When I want your opinion I'll give it to you.") Whether your tone is threatening or patronizing, your message is the same: You've got the floor and you're not giving it up. Certainly not to your partner. You may repeat yourself simply to maintain your "rights" as speaker. Domineering speech may be very slow and deliberate, indicating that you're adamant about your point of view and nothing is going to change it. Or your tone may be condescending, indicating that your partner is a simple child who needs to be shown the right way.

Belligerent talk lets your partner know you're really ready to fight. At the very least, you want to get a rise out of him or her. Phrases like, "Do you have an attitude problem or what?" "What is it *now?*" "Just trying to get on my nerves, is that it?" "What have you got to say for yourself?" "What's your complaint? Speak up!" are signs of this bullying.

If you recognize yourself in the description of belligerent or domineering speaking (or if your spouse recognizes you), you must work especially hard *not* to talk this way during arguments. No matter what justifications you may believe you have for these responses, the reality is that you will never be able to communicate effectively if you subject your mate to blatant or veiled threats.

Training yourself to speak to your spouse in a way that doesn't trigger a negative response will greatly cut down on your mate's defensiveness, which can only improve the communication between you. But it isn't enough. After all, at times when you'll be on the receiving end of a destructive, negative statement or look from your spouse, what do you do then? Most people reflexively become defensive in an attempt to ward off the attack. But as I'm sure you know by now, such phrases usually have the opposite effect, dragging you both further into a quagmire of accusations and hurt feelings.

When you're responding to a less-than-perfect comment from your spouse it's up to you to extricate both of you from a nasty, counterproductive confrontation. To do so, you need to avoid the defensive responses that we explored in chapter 3:

- Denying responsibility for a problem
- Making excuses
- Using phrases like "yes, but . . ."
- Whining
- Reacting to negative mind reading
- Cross-complaining
- Using the "rubber man" or "rubber woman" ploy
- Falling back on the repeating-yourself syndrome

Instead, try to respond in a way that lets your spouse know you're considering his or her perspective, even if you don't agree with it.

Below are some very defensive exchanges for which I have put more productive alternative statements in parentheses. I hope this will give you an idea about how to rewrite your own conversations. You may want to look over these examples with your spouse:

Example #1

WIFE: You never told me that your father was coming to visit us this weekend.

HUSBAND: I did so! (Alternative: "I thought I told you, but maybe I didn't. Sorry.")

WIFE: You did not! (Alternative: "Well, maybe you did and I didn't register it.")

HUSBAND: I did! (Alternative: "This is ridiculous. I'll take the blame for not telling you. I've been under some stress lately, so it's possible I forgot.")

Example #2

WIFE: You never take me out anymore.

HUSBAND: Baloney. I take you out lots. (Alternative: "Well, if that's the way you feel, then that's awful. Let's do something about it. How about dinner and a movie this Saturday?")

Example #3

WIFE: You never take me out anymore.

HUSBAND: Well, maybe you're right, but didn't you say you'd first have to find another babysitter? (This yes-but is like saying, "Yes, you are right, but you are also wrong." Alternative: "Well, what about asking your sister to babysit this Saturday and taking in dinner and a movie?")

Example #4

WIFE: You need to recognize that you have a tendency to be late. Since we now only have one car and we have to go to work together, you have to get up earlier. I hate being late and letting Jane down.

HUSBAND: You have to realize that I'm a night person. (Alternative: "Yeah, I know how you feel about being late and I know you were upset that you disappointed Jane last week. It wasn't your fault. It is hard for me to get up at 6 A.M. because I'm a night person.")

STRATEGY #3: VALIDATION

Letting your spouse know in so many little ways that you understand him or her is one of the most powerful tools for healing your relationship. It is an antidote to several of the horsemen—criticism, contempt, and defensiveness. Instead of attacking or ignoring your partner's point of view, you try to see the problem from your partner's perspective, and show that you think that viewpoint may have some validity.

Validation is especially important for men who tend to respond to their wives' upset by becoming hyperrational. Rather than acknowledge the emotional content of their wife's words, they try to offer a practical solution to the problem being described. This can be quite well-meaning, but it too often misses the mark. If your wife is being extremely emotional she probably isn't interested in hearing advice. She mostly needs to know that you understand what she's *feeling*.

Validation is simply putting yourself in your partner's shoes and imagining his or her emotional state. It is then a simple matter to let your mate know that you understand those feelings and consider them valid, even if you don't share them. Validation is an amazingly effective technique. It's as if you opened the door to welcome your partner. When your partner feels validated, he or she will feel much more comfortable confiding in you, and much more open to hearing your perspective as well.

Validation is a real art and has many gradations. At the top of the scale is true empathy and understanding. This entails actually feeling a bit of what your partner is experiencing and being able to see the world through your partner's eyes. Expressing this deep empathy will show that you not only understand your partner's view of the world but his or her sense of self. Few things make a person feel more loved and valued. There are some specific ways you can add a high level of validation to your talks.

Take Responsibility. If your husband says he gets upset when you don't call to let him know you'll be home late from work, try answering with, "Gee, I really made you angry, didn't I?" You are acknowledging that your actions might have provoked your partner's response.

Apologize. Similarly, a straight-out apology is a very strong form of validation because it lets your partner know you consider his or her gripe valid and worth respecting. To apologize you don't have to always say, "I'm sorry." You can simply say, "I see what you mean. I was wrong." Everyone is wrong from time to time. However, admitting this in an argument can have very powerful results.

Compliment. Honestly praising your spouse for handling a situation well will go a long way. Especially when there is tension between you, reminding your partner (and yourself!) that you really admire him or her is likely to have a powerful, positive effect on the rest of your conversation.

Doing the Minimum. At first, you may not be able to muster these high forms of validation. Fortunately, even a relatively minor type of validation, simply listening to and acknowledging your partner's point of view even if you don't share it, can work wonders. This type of validation can be as straightforward as saying, "Yes, I know that upsets you," when your husband says he's concerned about the children's grades. Be careful, however, not to end the sentence by harping on the fact that you don't agree. Do this and you'll cancel out the validation. Right now, your job isn't to argue for your point but to let your partner know you understand his or hers.

To see what an enormous difference a little bit of validation can make, consider the following discussion between Ward and Bridget. Both are unhappy with how things go between them when Ward gets home after a hard day's work.

Bridget's complaint is that Ward's only interest is to be fed dinner. She's exhausted after tending to the kids all day, running errands, etc. Rather than adding to her work load, she wants him to take care of *her* when he gets home—engage in adult conversation, maybe bring her flowers on occasion—or at least express interest in her thoughts or let her know he finds her attractive.

From Ward's perspective, he's exhausted at the end of the day and just wants to unwind. He'd like to relax, have his dinner, be given some peace and quiet, and have his wife express happiness that he's home. Being fed dinner makes him feel taken care of. It's a sign to him of Bridget's affection, that she's glad to see him. It's also the only time that the entire family spends together. He looks forward to this after a long, grueling day.

If Bridget and Ward attempted to discuss this conflict without expressing any validation, here's what their talk would sound like:

BRIDGET: You come home and right away you want supper.

WARD: At the end of a day usually I'm tired and I just want to unwind.

BRIDGET: And I've been home all day with the kids, and I've had it up to here, errands all day, no time for myself, and I look forward to your coming home so I can get a little relief.

WARD: I want to be left alone for a few minutes. I'd appreciate a little peace and quiet when I walk in the door.

BRIDGET: I want someone to take care of *me* for a change. I'd like some adult conversation.

WARD: I'd like a little concern or affection, or a sense that you're glad to see me.

BRIDGET: I want to feel that my husband will be interested in my thoughts or find me attractive or do something special for me.

WARD: I come home after a lot of tension all day and I want to relax. A home is a place you can unwind, and I want my wife to be interested in me and ask me how my day was.

BRIDGET: I'd like a little romance, like having you bring me flowers or tell me I look nice.

WARD: The meal is important to me. It makes me feel taken care of, and it's the one time we are all together as a family.

While reading this dialogue you could probably feel the tension increase as Bridget and Ward barreled ahead without recognizing each other's feelings or point of view. Now, here's the same dialogue, with each partner adding a touch of validation—just doing the min-imum.

BRIDGET: You come home and right away you want supper.

WARD: I can see how that would feel like just another demand in a long list you've had to deal with all day. Me, at the end of a day, usually I'm tired and I just want to unwind.

BRIDGET: I know that you've had a hard day on your feet with all that tension. And I've been home all day with the kids, and I've had it up to here, errands all day, no time for myself, and I look forward to your coming home so I can get a little relief.

WARD: I've been looking forward to seeing you, too. But to tell you the truth, I want to be left alone for a few minutes. I'd appreciate a little peace and quiet when I walk in the door.

BRIDGET: You need a little breathing room to unwind when you first walk in. And here I'm thinking I want someone to take care of *me* for a change instead of me doing for someone else all day long, and maybe having some adult conversation. Maybe you can do that once you've had a little breathing room, a chance to unwind.

WARD: Yeah, that would be great. I can see why you want someone taking care of you at the end of a day. Those kids can be pretty demanding. We need to provide some relief for each other. I can do that after I've relaxed for a few minutes. I also want a little concern and affection, to know you're glad to see me.

BRIDGET: I am glad to see you. But to tell you the truth, it would make me happy if you sounded interested in my thoughts or said you found me attractive or did something special for me.

WARD: Yeah, I can see that. I could think to bring you flowers. I have thought of it, really I have. Then I just get wrapped up with my own problems. I come home after a lot of tension all day and I want to relax. A home is a place you can unwind, and I want my wife to be interested in me and ask me how was my day.

BRIDGET: We're both needy at the end of a day.

WARD: Yeah. You know, the meal is important to me because it makes me feel taken care of, and it's one time when we are all together as a family and it means a lot to me to have dinner ready when I get home.

These two conversations are worlds apart in how they leave Bridget and Ward feeling. Yet the only difference between them is a small amount of validation.

If your relationship suffers from a high level of negativity, being able to acknowledge your partner's feelings may be more than you can muster right now. In that case you may find it encouraging to know that even a begrudging acceptance of your spouse's point of view is a form of validating. So even if you can't drum up an enthusiastic tone of voice, it's worth attempting to validate your spouse.

If, no matter how hard you try, you just can't see your partner's point of view, let him or her know that you're trying. You can simply say, "Right now, I'm just taking in what you're saying and attempting to understand how you feel." This at least conveys that you're giving it your best shot. Remember, though, that you can't fake validation. It must be genuine to be effective.

If you need extra motivation to try to empathize with your spouse during tough times, keep in mind that all this psychological and emotional awareness is good for your physical health. Research has clearly demonstrated that when you validate your spouse, you're helping to keep your blood pressure down and your heart rate from skyrocketing. In one study of newlyweds I found that adrenaline secretions decreased during a conversation if a couple were validating and positive toward each other. But couples who were not validating tended to secrete more and more adrenaline as their conversation progressed—and their tension rose.

STRATEGY #4: OVERLEARNING—TRY AND TRY AGAIN

When you've had one successful fight using these techniques, you may think you've mastered the strategies. I'm afraid there's more work involved. In fact, the worst thing you could do is to read this chapter once and never look at it again. It's not enough to have an intellectual understanding of "fighting smart." These lessons have to be practiced *often*. So often, in fact, that they become almost automatic.

This is true when you learn any new skill. You didn't just sail out of the driveway the first time you learned to drive; you didn't lob the ball neatly over the net the first time you played tennis; no doubt your first chocolate souffle did not rise evenly.

A colleague of mine told me the story of a couple she had seen in therapy for some time. Their marriage had been very troubled, but in this case she decided to teach the couple only one thing: for Sue, the wife, to become more aware that her husband Luke felt like running away from her strong statements of negativity, and for Luke to not run away but to stay and listen nondefensively. Several months after the therapy was over she visited this couple in their home to find out how they were doing. They had had a fight just before she came over. Luke said that they had fought while they were loading the dishwasher and he said that he had to work not to run out of the kitchen, his usual automatic impulse. At first he thought, "Why does Sue have to go and ruin a nice dinner we just had by bringing up some damned stupid grievance just now?" But he calmed himself down and said to himself, "Hang in there, Luke old boy, she's not all that mad." And he stayed and listened nondefensively. Sue also said that she had to work on her knowledge of his patterns and to soften her anger a bit. With every fight it got a little easier, and they eventually reported great improvements in their happiness together.

Each time you rehearse being nondefensive or validating is new and different and it's important to keep trying, even when you're tired and don't feel like it. Eventually these strategies will become more automatic. The best way to incorporate the principles outlined in this chapter is to rehearse them. Start small. For example, try some non-defensive speaking when you're talking about something innocuous like dinner, washing the car, or which video to rent.

You and your spouse have to practice these skills even when you don't necessarily feel like it. That means when you are tired, hungry, distracted, happy, sad, driving, watching TV, showering together—under all circumstances and conditions until it becomes a natural, effortless part of your interactions. You have to make it your own, imbue it with your own sense of humor, style, and personality. Then just keep doing it again and again. Keep clocking up the hours using the skill.

The idea is that if you overlearn a communication skill, you'll have access to it when you need it most—during an argument or heated fight when you are physiologically aroused. That's when all of this overlearning will pay off.

If you practice, practice, practice these skills you will have gone a very long way toward improving your marriage. It has been my experience that these four principles—*calming down, communicating nondefensively, validating,* and *overlearning*—are all that most marriages need in order to get back on track. I believe this is even true of marriages that have been almost completely subsumed by negativity. I don't mean to imply that you will see changes overnight, or that transforming your marriage will be easy. But if you are motivated, work hard, and don't let every setback discourage you, over time you will find your marriage a far happier place to be.

EIGHT

STRENGTHENING
THE FOUNDATIONS

T he foundation of a lasting marriage rests on two kinds
of bedrock: agreeing with your spouse on which style for handling
disagreements you both can live with, and a large dose of positivity.
This chapter gives you some final advice on these essential ingredients.

NEGOTIATING YOUR MARITAL STYLE

Many couples whose marriages are in difficulty were unable from
the start to negotiate their way to one of the three stable marriages. If
this is the case in your marriage—if you and your partner have never
managed to agree on the marital style you both prefer—then there
will be a subtext to every argument you have. That undercurrent will
be about *how* to argue, *how* to express and handle emotions between
you, *how* to feel loved and show love—in short, about what being
truly involved really means. With that undercurrent, hurt feelings,

resentments, rejection, and bitterness build. One of you may feel flooded, the other lonely; one attacked, the other unlistened to.

The tests in chapter 2 can help you get a clearer picture of which kind of marriage you prefer, and to see which kind of marriage your spouse is most comfortable in. If there is a great discrepancy—if you don't yet agree on which style or combination of styles feels right—then your marriage will benefit if you talk that over directly. To review, here are some guiding principles that may help you both decide which marital style for handling disagreements suits you best:

- *Togetherness vs. separateness.* If you strongly value "we-ness" more than your separateness and individuality, then you probably would be more comfortable with a validating style. If, on the other hand, you feel your own autonomy and separateness is more important, you may prefer a volatile or avoider style; couples in these marriages, for example, are more likely to have separate spaces in their homes that are purely his or hers, separate friends, and so on.

- *Romance and companionship.* If you highly value keeping your relationship dynamic and romantic, a volatile style may suit you. Validating couples are most concerned about being good companions and each other's best friend.

- *Honesty.* Bald frankness is a hallmark of volatile couples, who generally value being completely honest with each other, and don't believe in hiding negative feelings or their grievances on issues. They see honesty as the basis of their trust. Validating and avoiding couples, on the other hand, pick and choose when and on what issues they will be completely honest, and often underplay their expressions of negativity.

- *Persuasion.* Volatile couples feel that their partner is not really engaged with them if there is not a really involved give and take, and an active discussion of disagreements. Validating and avoiding couples value this kind of involvement far less.

- *Expressing emotion.* If you are very expressive emotionally, and prefer that in discussing marital conflicts, then the volatile style suits you. If you do, but in moderation, then the validating style is more likely your preference. And if you don't feel very comfortable with expressing strong negative feelings, you would probably prefer an avoiding style.

● *Traditional roles.* Validating and avoiding couples tend to prefer traditional sex roles in dividing up household tasks and child care.

● *Philosophy and beliefs.* Those in avoiding marriages are more likely than the other two styles to put a high value on having a shared set of religious or philosophical beliefs that guide their life together.

Much of the following advice can help any couple. But some types of marriage require more work in certain areas than others. That's because different types of stable marriages face different risks. With that in mind, I've developed a separate set of strategies for each of the three stable styles of marriage. Realize, though, that you can also adopt advice from the other two types from time to time, as you move through life's changes. (If your marriage is a hybrid type, you'll inevitably want to do this.) A volatile couple trying to cope with one partner's illness, for example, might find it helpful to behave like a conflict-avoiding couple, at least for a while. Once the crisis is over, however, they'll probably be more comfortable returning to their natural volatile approach to marriage.

ADVICE FOR VALIDATING COUPLES

This type of partnership has many strengths that you should be sure to build on—especially your great skills at negotiation and compromise. You and your spouse may get angry with one another from time to time, but you don't let bad feelings overtake the relationship. You often describe your spouse as your "best friend," and you emphasize warmth and sharing in your marriage. Therefore, you should practice a fighting style that honors and protects your friendship. Here are some tips:

Pick Your Battles Carefully. Don't sweat the small stuff, but don't run away from issues that have potential for making a good relationship better once they're resolved. For example, you may choose to let go of an occasional disagreement with your spouse over what to watch on television. But if you feel you're constantly competing with the TV for your spouse's attention, it may be time to confront this issue head-on.

Acknowledge Your Spouse's Viewpoint Before Expressing Your Own. This is particularly important for setting a productive stage for the agenda-building portion of the argument. It can be done by paraphrasing what your partner has just said, or through simple, encouraging words, gestures, and facial expressions.

Moderate Your Emotions. Try to stay on an even keel, particularly when you get to the persuasion segment of a fight. Too much anger or sadness may appear to threaten the foundation of your friendship.

Trust Your Partner. Since you two have a good understanding of one another emotionally, you can generally accept your spouse's "mind-reading" statements as valid, helpful insights into what you're experiencing. You'll also do well to accept your spouse's attempts to keep communication flowing. And when it comes time to find a solution, have an open mind. Continue to view the person across the table as your ally, a kindred spirit who has your best interests at heart.

Enhance Romance. Be on the lookout for a hazard that zaps the vitality out of many validating marriages—the demise of romance. Relentlessly seeking happy compromises can sap the sizzle out of a marriage, leaving you feeling more like buddies than lovers. This is especially true as couples move through major life transitions, such as becoming parents. The antidote is to take plenty of time out to nurture your marriage. Seek shared experiences that ignite your passion for one another. (We'll explore ideas on how to do this later in the chapter.)

ADVICE FOR VOLATILE COUPLES

Lack of sizzle is no problem for your marriage. If you're part of a volatile relationship, you feel a strong romantic attachment to your partner, and you're quite adept at juggling intense emotions like jealousy and anger. Such unions offer a big payoff in terms of romance, laughter, and affection. But unbridled passion can also put you at risk for contempt—or even violence—that could destroy your marriage.

That's why volatile couples should learn to "edit" their thoughts, words, and behavior on occasion. The idea is not to retreat from a good, healthy battle, but to handle conflict in a way that demonstrates respect for your opponent. Otherwise you may lose the high ratio of positive interaction in your relationship. To that end, consider my seven "editorial tips for politeness":

Don't Tell Your Partner What You Can't or Won't Do. Instead, emphasize what you *can* and *want* to do. For instance, if your spouse requests that you come along on a household shopping expedition, your first thought might be: "I've got a million things to do today. There's no way I can spend more than two hours on this trivia." Take a second to edit your statement before you utter it, so you highlight the positive part: "I've got two hours I can go shopping today, from three o'clock to five. Let's do it." The outcome is essentially the same, but the communication around it is much friendlier.

Offer Sincere and Positive Appreciation. With a little effort and empathy, you can replace thoughtless complaints and criticism with thoughtful remarks. If your partner overcooks your morning omelet, comment on the fresh-squeezed orange juice rather than the shriveled eggs. By focusing on what you think your spouse most wants and deserves to hear from you in this situation, you can offer thanks instead of criticism. If you can't think of *anything* nice to say in a particular situation, try asking your spouse what he or she would most like to hear. Similarly, you can help your spouse to please you by revealing what you need as well.

I'm not advising volatile couples to avoid talking about significant conflicts. But such discussions may be more productive if they take place in an atmosphere of appreciation and respect.

While disagreement is important in volatile couples, they're not mean-spirited relationships—remember that volatile couples are usually the most affectionate and romantic, too. Being more affectionate, offering sincere thanks, and showing appreciation is more characteristic of happily married volatile couples than it is of the less happily married ones. It's quite simple to sprinkle tokens of appreciation in your interactions, for example:

"I appreciate your raising this issue."

"I respect your honesty."

"Thanks for taking Jason to buy a new quilt."

"I loved the flowers."

"I appreciate your telling Eve a goodnight story tonight."

"I'm grateful that I got to go to that class tonight. Thanks."

Express Interest in Your Spouse. It's often easy for partners to be preoccupied with their own thoughts and interests. But you can build rapport and show respect for your spouse by asking questions about one another's jobs, hobbies, friends, etc. Be attentive to the responses you get. Tune in to one another's ideas and avoid unnecessary interruptions.

Choose to Be Polite, Regardless of Your Spouse's Actions. Volatile couples, in particular, risk falling into a trap of negative reciprocity—that is, exchanging one criticism or insult for another. But if just one of you commits to responding with consideration, no matter how the other reacts, you may be able to avoid a chain of negativity that can threaten marital stability. Since politeness vanishes early on in a marriage, even among happily married newlyweds, purposely treating your spouse as nicely and with the consideration you treat a stranger is a real option for making things better.

Be Direct and Honest. Because truthfulness is highly valued in a volatile marriage, it's important that you both feel free to ventilate your emotions. This style of marriage thrives on conflict, so don't hold back when trying to persuade your partner. You can win respect by meeting fire with fire. At the same time, you must guard against the four horsemen that can take you on a swift ride toward divorce. Confront your spouse face-to-face, but be prepared to back off if you sense your attack has become too painful or humiliating.

Teasing and direct confrontation have positive results in a volatile marriage, but they can go too far. Here's an example of backing off at the right time:

WIFE: They're my parents and I want you to treat them with respect.

HUSBAND: But I don't respect them.

WIFE: So you disappear when we visit.

HUSBAND: Yeah, at least that way I don't get rude.

WIFE: Yes you do.

HUSBAND: Only at dinner when your stupid father gets philosophical.

WIFE: He's not stupid. He raised a bunch of children and worked hard all his life. He's just not that educated.

HUSBAND: He's stupid and you know it.

WIFE: (*In tears*) You don't respect anybody!

HUSBAND: You're right, I'm too smug. It works when I debate other lawyers, but you're right, he does deserve my respect for having raised a wonderful wife for me. I'll try to be more civil this Thanksgiving. [He sees he's gone too far and backs off.]

WIFE: Thanks.

HUSBAND: Don't expect too much.

WIFE: I won't but I appreciate your trying.

Affection. Here's that word again! Don't assume your spouse knows you love and admire him or her. You need to communicate it frequently. Affection is especially important in the volatile marriage— it's the key to marital happiness. Here's a conversation between two people in a volatile marriage where there is a lot of affection:

WIFE: I'll never get that promotion. I'm just not aggressive enough.

HUSBAND: I think of you as a short barracuda myself.

WIFE: With you I am. But that Roger Priestly will beat me out.

HUSBAND: There's no way you won't get this promotion. You are so incredibly competent and cute. And you are the one they owe the San Francisco job to. Roger is so vain.

WIFE: Doesn't matter. No one notices what a jerk he is but you and me. Fred never has seen that side of Roger.

HUSBAND: Okay, let's hatch a plan to destroy Roger. I've got it. Every day you come in and you subtly build up his ego, get him talking about himself and tell him that Fred will find that story fascinating. Pretty soon he's spending all his time bragging to Freddie.

WIFE: And Freddie hates that. It might work. Did you know the other day he spent twenty minutes talking about himself and he never asked me a single thing about me! That bore!

HUSBAND: Men! I hate men!

WIFE: All except you.

HUSBAND: (*Laughs*) That's why I'm a liberated man. Cause I love women (*laughs*).

WIFE: (*Laughs*) You're as sexist as they come.

Be Careful About Teasing. Although razzing your mate can be playful and a sign of affection, if you're feeling defensive that gentle ribbing can turn into painful poking. Teasing is damaging when it is hostile and negative.

ADVICE FOR CONFLICT-AVOIDING COUPLES

One of the greatest strengths of a conflict-avoiding marriage is the ability to endure periodic turbulence based on the certainty that your relationship is built on a rock-solid foundation of common beliefs and values. But, while you may cherish the peaceful nature of your relationship above all else, you could be stifling too much negative emotion and not getting your needs met as individuals. When this happens, you risk becoming hostile and detached from one another. Some psychologists even theorize that conflict-avoiding couples suffer more physical ailments than others as a result of living with unresolved problems. If you turn all negative feelings inward, you're left with chronic, low-lying stress that eats away at your health and the stability of your marriage.

Does this mean conflict-avoiding couples should transform their marriage into a version of "The Lockhorns"? Hardly. Inviting turmoil into a marriage before you've developed good conflict-management skills could even be dangerous. But there are steps you can take to improve your ability to handle the negative feelings that inevitably crop up in any partnership. By so doing, you improve the likelihood that your bond will remain stable.

Get in Touch with Your Feelings. Solving problems in a relationship usually requires partners to talk about their negative feelings. But that's hard if you both tend to cover up or ignore emotional cues. Some people fear that letting out negative emotions like anger, rage, jealousy, fear, or sorrow will lead to catastrophe, such as the loss of their partner's respect or even divorce. It may help if you remember that it's not necessary to always win your partner's approval. Sometimes, especially during a crisis, it's more important to express what you're feeling. Acknowledging your emotions will *not* cause you to lose control over who you are and how you behave.

If you are not the type of person who has focused much on your emotions, it may take some practice before you can easily identify, much less articulate, what you're feeling. Recognizing physical cues and thought patterns that typically accompany specific feelings can help. Take a look at the chart below to identify what you're feeling at any given moment. Go over it from time to time and see how your responses vary.

POSITIVE FEELINGS
I feel (a little, somewhat, very):

relaxed	content
calm	loving
glowing	bubbly
warm	peaceful
sexy	confident
excited	interested
willing	intrigued
secure	ambitious
strong	imaginative
happy	creative
busy	intimate

NEGATIVE FEELINGS

I feel (a little, somewhat, very):

grouchy	shy
sad	hurt
anxious	guilty
tired	frustrated
nervous	sorry
ashamed	incompetent
bored	rebellious
lonely	confused
dumb	listless
trapped	depressed
put down	restless
silly	hungry

After you make your selection, notice the physical signals accompanying that emotion. Can you feel tension in specific muscle groups? In your neck? Hands? Jaw? Chest? Gut? Is it hard to talk? Is your mouth dry? Are you sweating? Keep a diary of your physical cues. At the same time, consider the thoughts that led to this emotion. Make a record of what you were thinking as you experienced each feeling. Then study your notes from time to time. Eventually, you may learn to read and express your emotions more easily.

Reaffirm Your Basic Beliefs About Your Relationship. During rocky times many conflict-avoiding couples find strength by reminding themselves of how similarly they view their relationship. To remind yourself of your bond, ask yourself questions like: What beliefs do we share about the strength of our marriage? What rules of conflict do we subscribe to? How have we agreed to make decisions within our relationship? What do we believe are the proper roles for husbands and wives? Answering these questions together may give you the security you need when your relationship is headed for stormy waters. Carl and Beth, for example, are part of a spiritual community that places a high value on keeping marriages together. In therapy recently to resolve sexual differences, the couple was able to express uncomfortable feelings of sadness and anger by reminding themselves that, no matter what, theirs was a marriage sanctified by God; their faith would help them find a way to solve their problems and stay married. Others may find similar support by reflecting on the particular beliefs or support systems that drew and keep them together.

Learn to Level with Your Spouse When Necessary. Tackling sensitive issues can be frightening if you've spent most of your relationship shying away from problems rather than facing them. But by focusing on the long-term well-being of your relationship, you may find the courage to address issues that pose the greatest threats. You can learn to level with your spouse in an honest, loving way by practicing the nondefensive speaking and listening techniques described earlier. Keep in mind that you can always seek the help of clergy or a professional marriage counselor if it feels like your conflicts are getting out of hand.

Avoiders can level by restating their feelings. You still minimize the severity of the issue, but you keep bringing up the subject, and don't pretend that you have no negative feelings about the subject. You can do this by focusing on the long range picture, and doing it gently. Eventually you will drift into a solution to the problems. You can, for example, think of someone else who had this problem and what they did, or think of some approach to the problem (perhaps based on religious advice or something in the Bible) that your partner would like. Usually avoiders face the problem together, shoulder to shoulder, and find an indirect approach to solving the problem. Here is an example:

HUSBAND: Couldn't we afford to get recessed lights?

WIFE: Dad doesn't like them and he's paying the bills for the remodeling.

HUSBAND: I wish there were a way we could afford the recessed lights.

WIFE: So do I. But the rest of the remodel is going okay, don't you think?

HUSBAND: Oh yeah sure. Your dad's a great guy and very generous, but . . .

WIFE: You want recessed . . .

HUSBAND: . . . lights. Yeah I do.

WIFE: What about doing what the Parkinsons did?

HUSBAND: What was that?

WIFE: They got a small bridge loan.

HUSBAND: Wouldn't your dad hate us doing that?

WIFE: Let's not tell him.

HUSBAND: I could talk to the contractor.

WIFE: Let's do it.

HUSBAND: It has been a great remodel.

WIFE: Yeah. Some people say it's so awful.

HUSBAND: Hasn't been for us.

WIFE: True.

This would have been a very mild way of leveling for a volatile couple, and wouldn't have worked for them. But it works very well in an avoiding marriage. It's persistent enough and it still contains plenty of reaffirming of the marriage.

Create "Suggestion Boxes." Businesses have used this technique to surface sensitive issues from their customers and employees for years; it may help you level with your spouse, as well. Take two boxes—one for you and one for your spouse—and label each "suggestion box." Then write down issues that are bothering you and deposit them into one another's boxes. There are two rules: First, don't fish out a suggestion unless you're ready and willing to hear how your spouse is feeling. Second, schedule a time when the two of you can talk without being defensive. It may be helpful to review the guidelines for non-defensive communication before you write out your suggestions or discuss them.

Turn to Others for Support. Friends and relatives outside your immediate family may help you to express and work through negative feelings about your marriage. Find a person or a support group you trust and use them as a sounding board when troubles arise.

PRODUCTIVE DISAGREEMENTS: GOOD FOR ALL MARRIAGES

Apart from these tips for handling disagreements that are specific to one of the three stable marriage types, there are some general points that apply to all couples—especially those where partners tend to feel flooded or act defensive. If this is the case in your marriage, you can be helped with your discussions of hot topics by imposing some intentional structure and through methods that will help deescalate the topics. Here are specific ways to do that.

SCHEDULE DISCUSSIONS

Scheduling discussions is particularly important for couples who have entered a cycle of negativity or the Distance and Isolation Cascade. These are points at which you may be feeling that your unresolved problems are overwhelming, leaving you feeling desperate and hopeless. Knowing that a discussion is scheduled at least gives you certainty that you both acknowledge there is a need to talk and have agreed on a time to do so.

And, apart from these problems, you may find it's easier to keep your arguments constructive if you earmark specific times to discuss difficult subjects. Knowing you have a set appointment to talk will prevent you from stewing over a problem or holding things in until you burst. By setting aside a specific amount of time (twenty minutes is a good, general guideline), you don't have to worry that the discussion will be endless. You can even plan ahead to go to a movie or fix dinner when you're done. Be sure you choose a time when you'll both be fairly rested and relaxed and can keep interruptions to a minimum. Often, couples tell me that Sunday afternoon is a good time for such talks.

At the beginning of your weekly discussion set the agenda. Pick only one issue so you don't start "kitchen-sinking" and get off track or overwhelmed. If you have more than one issue to discuss, schedule more appointments for later in the week.

I admit that allocating a time and setting an agenda may sound more appropriate for a business relationship than a marriage. I wish I could offer you some snappy solutions for overcoming the artificiality of this arrangement, but there aren't any. All I can tell you is that this approach works well for most couples. I recognize how awkward it may feel at first, but this structuring does help prevent arguments from getting off beam.

Be prepared for the occasions when you and your spouse fall off schedule. For example, a fight about refinancing the house may erupt before your appointment to talk about it. Force yourselves to call a halt to your discussion until the preordained time, or, if it is urgent, make sure you set aside enough time to talk immediately. Don't try to have an important discussion on the run. This may require enormous willpower, but it's worth it.

As you get closer to the time of your appointment, one or both of you may feel less and less like talking. Men, especially, tend to get physiologically aroused as the dreaded hour approaches. This is quite understandable. Try to remember that you're having these meetings to keep your marriage healthy. It's just like going to the dentist. It's hardly pleasant, but the benefits should make it bearable.

STRUCTURE YOUR FIGHTS

As I've already mentioned, people in stable marriages usually go through three stages when they argue. Once they focus on what to discuss, they hear each other out, validating their spouse's point of view. Next, each partner tries to persuade the other to see things his or her way. Finally, they reach an agreement on how to resolve the conflict. Our research shows that most couples experience all three stages when they argue, but spend differing amounts of time in each depending on their marital style. Validating couples spend a good deal of time listening and empathizing. Volatile couples tend to jump into the persuasion phase very quickly, while conflict-avoiding couples may try to skip over this stage and head straight for a resolution. Regardless of your marital style, there are techniques for making each stage of conflict as productive as possible.

Phase One: Building the Agenda. Here, the task is to first focus the discussion on a specific issue. Although you may be tempted to address everything from unpaid bills to your mother-in-law's personality, you'll get better results if you stick to one topic. Exploding with a kitchen-sinking complaint like "I'm fed up with this messy house, our boring sex life, and your constant spending" only confuses and stalls the process.

Make sure each of you gets a chance to state your point of view during this early stage of the argument. This will help to ensure that the discussion remains balanced later on. The agenda-building phase is also a perfect time for couples to validate one another's perspectives. Remember that validation doesn't necessarily mean that you agree with what your partner is saying. But it gives you the chance to show that you respect your spouse's feelings and can understand how it's possible that he or she would hold a particular opinion.

Validation can be as simple as communicating to your partner that you are "tracking," that is, listening and taking in your partner's point of view. But this kind of active listening isn't easy when you're upset and don't share your partner's viewpoint. At a minimum you can try the simple exercise of paraphrasing what you think your partner is saying, without judgment, and then check it out. This simple exercise will go a long way to starting the process of validating.

> HUSBAND: I'm just tired of wasting our weekends. Let's plan something that's fun.
>
> WIFE: You want us to have weekend plans.
>
> HUSBAND: That's right, plans that are enjoyable, not just running errands.
>
> WIFE: You want to get away from the drudgery. You're tired of it and want more fun on the weekends.
>
> HUSBAND: Exactly.

Ultimately the goal of validation is genuine empathy. Empathy is not only *hearing* what your partner is saying but understanding the *feelings* behind it.

Phase Two: Persuasion and Arguing. Once you've set the agenda and listened to each other's perspectives, the next stage usually entails trying to persuade your partner that your approach to the problem is better. Since this phase can get quite hot emotionally, it's prime time to practice repair mechanisms (humor, affection, empathy, etc.) that you'll learn about later in this chapter. It's also the perfect opportunity to use the nondefensive communication skills we've explored in chapter 7. As long as you keep listening closely to each other's point of view, this phase won't degenerate into unproductive squabbling. Rather, it should lead you to the next step: finding a compromise.

Phase Three: Resolution. After you have delivered your best persuasive arguments, start working on a peace plan. The goal is to come up with a solution that is satisfying, or at least acceptable, to both of you.

Look for opportunities to compromise. Reflecting on the values and beliefs you share as a couple can be a real help. Compromise also comes easier if you listen carefully to your partner's suggestions and try to find ways to build upon them and suit both your needs. Dave, for example, wanted to spend summer vacation fly fishing, so he suggested a family camping trip to his favorite fishing spot. Getting out of town sounded good to Louise, but she preferred more creature comforts than camping allowed. She countered with a suggestion that they rent a cabin near the river. This sounded like a reasonable compromise to Dave, but he was concerned that the cabin would cost too much. After some discussion, they agreed to cut back on other luxuries for a while to make renting the cabin possible.

Emphasizing the positive aspects of your marriage can be helpful when searching out a resolution. Imagine what a difference it makes if Louise says, "We really have a great time together when we go places where we can *both* relax," versus a defensive statement, "You never think about the kind of vacation *I'd* like to have."

Once you're close to finding a compromise, make sure you are both genuinely satisfied with it. Faking acceptance just to be done with a tedious or uncomfortable discussion usually backfires because the unresolved issue will probably crop up again and again.

NONDEFENSIVE COMMUNICATION

Here's help if defensiveness is a problem for you. For many couples, wide-ranging strategies like reading body language or using validation and XYZ statements are enough to overcome defensiveness when trying to work out a touchy issue. But many others get stuck in one or more of the specific types of defensive speaking patterns that I described in chapter 3. If that sounds like you or your spouse, the advice below, geared to particular defensive maneuvers, can help you out of the rut.

Solution to Denying Responsibility. Fess up and be accountable. Try saying, "Gee, I guess I was wrong there" or, "I really shouldn't have done that." Maybe even, "You're right, that's a good point." Any of these acknowledge that you know you made a mistake and will try not to do it again.

Solution to Cross-Complaining. Remember that arguments are most constructive if you only discuss one issue at a time. If you can refrain from answering each of your partner's complaints with a complaint of your own, your differences will be resolved far more easily. It may feel unfair to you to have to hold off on your gripe until later. But if you extend your spouse this courtesy, he or she will eventually reciprocate. This is the best way to break the cross-complaining deadlock.

Solution to Whining. There is no clever alternative to whining. The solution is simple: don't do it. Before you speak, count to ten, or even a hundred, bite your tongue, or take a deep breath. Instead of whining, explain in a straightforward way why you feel like you're being picked on.

Solution to Rubber Man or Woman. If you instinctively throw back at your spouse accusations directed at you, try instead to acknowledge that you're not perfect and that maybe your partner has a point. You might be amazed to find that you share common ground. After all, if you're both accusing each other of the same "flaw," maybe there's a reason. So if your wife says you're irresponsible, own up. "Yeah, you're right. Sometimes I just don't want to be a grown-up." This leaves her room to acknowledge her own wish to abdicate adulthood. "Me neither. Sometimes I just want to chuck it all." Suddenly you're a team, working on the issue together rather than adversaries trying to load off all the blame on the other person.

Solution to Summarizing-Self Syndrome. If you sound like a broken record during arguments, making your point over and over again to a seemingly heedless spouse, try recapping your partner's perspective instead of your own. This is a form of validation that may break you out of this endless cycle. A similar approach is to summarize *both* of your viewpoints, emphasizing what you agree about: "I guess we both get upset because the house is messy." Or, "I guess it bothers both of us that we can't afford to take much of a vacation this year." Even, "Seems neither one of us likes it when I discipline Jason and then he runs to you for sympathy."

This sends the message that you see your marriage as a team effort and that you're approaching the problem with a we're-in-this-together spirit.

SOOTHE YOUR PARTNER: REPAIR MECHANISMS

Perhaps the most powerful way to break out of negative cycles—like attack and withdrawal, or contempt and stonewalling—that throw your settlement of disagreements off-track is to soothe your spouse. If you can recognize the signs that your partner is becoming upset, defensive, critical, or withdrawn, you can short-circuit the problem before it destroys your talk. This is especially important if your partner is prone to flooding; it is also a potent antidote to the cycle of negativity, because it makes it far less likely that you or your partner will reciprocate negativity with more hostility.

Here are some repair mechanisms you may find effective as strategies that keep negativity from getting out of hand. While they are useful at any time in a marriage, they offer special benefits during an argument that has grown too heated.

Stop Action. If your partner shows signs of imminent flooding, a good strategy is to call a "stop action." Unlike the "time-out" I discussed earlier, a "stop action" doesn't necessarily entail postponing your talk for twenty minutes or so while you calm down. The point is to call a "stop action" before that more intensive tactic becomes necessary. You can literally hold up your hand and announce: "Stop action!" This lets your mate know that you think one (or both) of you is in danger of flooding. What you do next depends on you. You may decide to call an official time-out, or opt for a quick back rub instead. In some cases, just announcing the stop action will be enough to let you regroup and get back on course. Think of it as pulling off to the side of the road to look at a map when you feel you've lost your way. If you do decide to take a time-out, remember to avoid returning to the discussion before your heart rates have dropped to baseline.

A stop action can short-circuit a conversation before it escalates to the point that one or both of you is flooded. The idea is to establish the rule that either of you can call "Time" and the conversation just stops dead in its tracks, to be resumed later. Here is an example:

> SUE: I feel like you are saying that the house is entirely my responsiblity, that I'm to blame if it's not up to your standards.
>
> JOE: Your stuff is everywhere.
>
> SUE: I go to school and take care of our daughter. Most people think it's amazing that I get so much done. All I hear from you is complaints.
>
> JOE: And all you're going to hear is complaints until you do what you agreed to do.
>
> SUE: I probably ought to drop out of school and just clean.
>
> JOE: Maybe.
>
> SUE: I won't give you that satisfaction. . . . I need a Stop Action. I am getting very upset here.
>
> JOE: All right, let's take a break.
>
> SUE: I think I'll go for a walk.
>
> JOE: Okay.

When Sue and Joe later returned to the topic, they had each had a chance to calm down and the conversation started on a better footing:

> JOE: Honey, I am sorry I got so mean. I'm really a strong supporter of your going to school and finishing your degree.
>
> SUE: I know you are. I'm sorry too.
>
> JOE: What can we do about straightening things up?
>
> SUE: Let's get a housecleaner.
>
> JOE: Great idea. How much would it cost?
>
> SUE: Once a week? Maybe a couple hundred a month.

JOE: That's too much.

SUE: It wouldn't be if I took that part-time job at the library.

JOE: Maybe that's a good idea.

Editing. When you edit you respond only to the constructive portions of your partner's comments and completely ignore the nasty tone of voice, insult, or criticism that accompanies it. This diffuses the tension, so you're more likely to refocus on the issue instead of the baggage that accompanies it.

For example, if your husband says, "Will you *stop* interrupting me, for God's sake?" your natural tendency may be to respond with a retort like, "I wouldn't have to interrupt if you didn't talk too much." But when you edit, you react only to the useful portion of his message: he wants you to allow him to speak. A calm reply like, "Okay, go ahead and finish what you were saying" will greatly diffuse the tension and get you back on track.

Another part of editing is to eliminate the negative in your response. For example, you may feel like saying, "Yes, I know you're upset that Susie is late, but if you hadn't been so pigheaded about scheduling the dinner too early she would have been here on time." When you edit, you delete the second half of that thought. All your partner hears is, "Yes, I know you're upset that Susie is late."

Gate-Keeping. Here, you give your partner directions that keep the discussion flowing in the right direction. This can be asking your spouse to continue talking, to elaborate, or to listen to you. Phrases like "go on," "tell me the story behind that," "stop interrupting me," and "I'm not finished" are examples of gate-keeping.

Getting Back on Beam. This is another way to keep the conversation on track and on topic. You explicitly alert you partner that you're drifting and call him or her back in. For example, saying, "That's off the subject. Let's stick to discussing the budget."

Affection. You may be tired of hearing this, but being understanding, empathetic, or validating is a profoundly effective way to repair communication. For example: "I want you to know you're not alone with this problem," "I like your idea," "I love you," "I understand how you feel."

Humor. No one can teach you how to be funny, but if you let yourself go, you may find yourself tickled by life's absurdities as well as your own. Humor starts with being able to laugh at yourself. It is a masterful way to diffuse a tense situation.

Conflict-Avoiding Techniques. Even if the conflict-avoidant type of marriage isn't right for you in general, you can learn a lot about soothing from this marital style. Conflict avoiders are great at gaining perspective on a dispute. They minimize the importance of the issue compared to all the good in their marriage. One way to do this is to appeal to your underlying shared philosophy. For example: "This just isn't very important to me compared to all the great things about our marriage," "I love a lot of things about our sex life," "We have really built a strong family."

Feeling Probes. Ask your spouse what he or she is feeling and then sit back and listen nondefensively for a while. Don't judge your mate's emotions or express disagreement with them.

Metacommunication. This is a complex term that simply means discussing how you're communicating. If you're getting off track, focusing on your interaction itself, rather than the specific topic under debate, can soothe you both. For example: "When you say that, it hurts my feelings," "Let's stop talking about the house and talk instead about how we're feeling right now."

Softening Persuasion Attempts. If you sense you're heading for gridlock, try backing off from taking a strong stand. For example: "Okay, maybe you're right about that. Can we find a middle ground?"

TAKING STOCK OF YOUR MARRIAGE

Of course, there's more to a lasting marriage than disagreements. To foster stable marriages, couples need to continually celebrate those areas where they can come together, and not let their inherent differences pull them down. To be sure, any marriage is made up of two individuals with differing needs, tastes, and interests. And you may wish at times that your partner was different—more outgoing or less social, more intellectually minded or less bookish, more this or less that. But you get into trouble when you try to re-create one another to fit your own ideals. Nobody wants to be coerced. Nobody wants to bear full responsibility for another's happiness. Our research shows that the happiest, most stable couples are those who accept that all marriages—and all spouses—have their limitations.

Think back to your childhood fantasies about marriage. Perhaps you dreamed that your trip to the altar would transform you, that once you were married, you would feel "complete as a person," and your spouse would fill your life with endless romance, happy music, and undying laughter. The sad part is that many people still cling to this fantasy. They expect their marriages to deliver total personal fulfillment and they find themselves disappointed when it doesn't happen.

If your marriage has been rocky, you may wonder, So just what are sufficient grounds for remaining married? While each couple must discover their own answer to this question, my research suggests some answers. At the very least, our studies show how extensive the grounds need to be. Remember that marital stability rests on a 5-to-1 ratio of good to bad times. Happy, solid couples nourish their marriages with plenty of positive moments together.

Learning to resolve conflict effectively is important to maintaining this ratio. But couples also need a proportionate measure of pleasure and joy in their marriages. Infusing your relationship with happy, shared experiences is especially important if you think your marriage is "basically okay" but boring. Couples flourish when they have a sense that they are creating something together—whether that's raising a family, building a business, or sharing a hobby. Too often, families lead complex—even grueling—lives in which they sacrifice the happy times for more materialistic, fleeting goals. Evenings in front of the fire give way to evenings in front of the television. Sundays at the office take the place of Sundays at the park. But if you want to keep your marriage alive, it's essential to rediscover—or perhaps simply make time for—those experiences that make you feel good about your spouse and your marriage.

Only you and your partner know what particular feelings and experiences can help to keep your marriage strong and vital. But I can offer two pieces of advice based on what I've observed among stable couples in my research. The first is to have realistic expectations about your marriage. The second is to treat your spouse with love and respect.

FINDING THE GLORY IN YOUR MARITAL STORY

One sure sign of a strong marriage is a couple's tendency to "glorify" the struggles they've been through together. In interviews, we found that a stable couple will describe their marriage in terms of a worthwhile journey, a saga in which they face adversity and become closer because of it. They tell detailed stories about certain traumas or intense experiences that bonded them to one another. They say they've come through troubled times feeling more committed and hopeful about their relationship.

It's not that couples who glorify their marriages actually faced more troubles than less stable pairs. But they seem to garner more meaning and inspiration from their hardships than others might.

One couple, for example, now looks back fondly on their newlywed days when the wife, Vicki, found herself having grave doubts about the decision to marry. You could imagine how such wavering could have deeply damaged a marriage. But Vicki and her husband Ben insist the crisis made their marriage stronger. Working through it made them all the more confident that their bond was real.

VICKI: Before the wedding I wasn't nervous or anything. I was ready to go. Then, after we got married I thought, "Wait a minute!" I got all upset thinking he wasn't the one, that I chose wrong. I had a really tough time with it, any little annoying thing he did just set me off. I kept threatening to leave him.

BEN: (*Laughs*) They were just the littlest, silly things.

VICKI: But then I would cry and really feel bad because I hurt him. He used to always sit in this old big, black chair. And I would go crawl on his lap and we'd talk about it and work it out.

BEN: Yeah, we always managed to work it out.

VICKI: After a while I just settled down and I began to see that he really was the neat guy I had dated. Soon it was terrific because we were together all the time. I got used to having him there, and that was what has been so special about our relationship ever since.

Another couple, Blanche and Murray, recall with pride the early lean years, when they lived on practically nothing but bean soup in a one-room apartment.

MURRAY: When it was just me, I lived fine working only part time. I paid for my own schooling and everything. But when we got married I started working full time because Blanche was in school. But even then it was just tough to make ends meet. It was a tough adjustment.

BLANCHE: He felt a real responsibility toward me—not wanting me to worry about where the next meal was gonna come from. It was hard to meet the bills, but we always made it.

What made matters worse was that Murray greatly disliked his job, but felt he couldn't quit. Yet, rather than recalling the misery of that period, what he most remembers is how supportive Blanche was.

MURRAY: She had to be patient with me while I was looking for other work. I'd come home and be grouchy, so she'd try to do things to cheer me up. She'd make fancier meals than just the usual boiled hot dogs. She'd try to jazz it up a little bit.

BLANCHE: And I'd write him little notes.

MURRAY: Right. Just little words of encouragement. That helped me. Pretty soon I was able to change my attitude. I accepted that the job I had was by no means permanent, I would find a different one eventually. And it's no use to let something that's not important upset you so much. So I took a different attitude. She helped and encouraged me to do that.

BLANCHE: I still write him notes!

MURRAY: We still go on dates. The other night we went and bought ice cream cones.

BLANCHE: That was fun. We do lots of just little fun things.

The point is that stable marriages become even stronger in the telling of the tale. Stable couples' stories serve to bolster their faith in one another and their union.

What about your marriage? What meaning and inspiration can you and your spouse find in the history of your relationship?

EXERCISE: TELLING YOUR STORY

This exercise is designed to help you and your partner find the glory in your marital story. The following questions are based on the oral history interview we use in our research. I have reworded some of the questions, however, in order to elicit favorable responses whenever possible. After all, the aim is to help reinforce positive beliefs and feelings about your marriage. So don't be afraid to put a positive spin on your responses, to say the glass is half full rather than half empty. (If, however, you find that the exercise only brings up negative feelings, don't despair. Just use the opportunity to talk about those feelings and try to determine why you don't feel better about your shared past. Were there conflicts you could have avoided? Episodes that you wish you'd handled better? Once you've identified these unsatisfactory aspects of your relationship, talk about ways you might change so that you'll feel better about similar issues in the future.)

Take time to read each question and jot down a few notes. Then, addressing one question at a time, discuss your answers with one another. Most of these questions are open-ended, allowing the respondents to answer with as much detail as they would like.

1. What was your first impression of your spouse? Was there something about this person that made him/her stand out?

2. Think back to the time you were dating. What were some of the highlights? What were some of the tensions? What made the relationship worth pursuing?

3. How did you decide to get married? Were there obvious differences that you knew you'd have to overcome? How did you overcome them?

4. What do you remember about your first year of marriage? Did

you have to make certain adjustments to being married? How did you do it?

5. What about your transition to becoming parents? What were the most difficult and most rewarding aspects of this period in your lives?

6. Looking back, what moments stand out as the really good times in your marriage so far?

7. Looking back, what moments stand out as the really hard times in your marriage so far? Why do you think you stayed together? How did you get through these difficult times?

8. How would you say your marriage today is different from when you first got married?

EXERCISE: HOW DO WE COMPARE?

This exercise gives you a chance to see the strengths of your marriage by comparing yourselves to other couples in your lives.

1. Each of you jot down the names of four different couples you both know. Two should be examples of "good" marriages; two should be examples of "bad" marriages.

2. Now share the names with one another and tell why you feel the good marriages work, and why the bad marriages don't. Perhaps you admire how the one couple is raising their children, for example. Or maybe you disapprove of the way another couple berates one another in front of company.

3. Talk about your own marriage in relation to these good and bad marriages. Compare the way you and your spouse manage to get through difficult times with the way each of these couples handle their challenges. Can you identify behaviors you want to avoid? Are there things you'd like to emulate?

4. Talk about your own ability as a couple to overcome hardship. Have you weathered episodes or incidents of which you're particularly proud? If so, how did you do it?

If you enjoy these exercises and find them helpful, you might consider doing them on a regular basis, perhaps around each wedding anniversary. This will give you a chance to reminisce about the past year as well as your ancient history.

I know one couple who keeps an up-to-date scrapbook of photos and memorabilia that celebrates their life together. They add to it in much the same way they do their daughter's baby book, using it to chronicle the life of their relationship. Included are snapshots from favorite vacations and family events, cards they've shared throughout the year, and silly notes they've jotted down for one another. The project gives them an excuse to collect physical evidence year-round of how their marriage works. Then, from time to time, they sit down and reflect on the happy times, reconfirming their commitment to one another.

I applaud couples who make such assertive efforts to keep their relationships lively. They're taking on the trickier task: they're continually establishing "grounds for marriage," and it makes their lives together all the richer.

KNOWING WHEN TO GET HELP, OR GIVE UP

I've stressed three simple ideas in this chapter: love, respect, and a sense of the value of your history together. If your marriage is utterly lacking in these—if you find it difficult to find much to admire in your spouse, or if you basically feel unrespected, if you find it hard to feel affection for your spouse, if you feel uncared for and unloved, and if when you look back on your marriage, it all seems pointless and wasted—then you ought to seriously consider ending your marriage.

Your options are to stick it out in spite of your feelings, to try to change your marriage, or end it. But before you make a leap of despair and end it, consider whether your bleak outlook might be because of something in your relationship that could be changed. That may be the case, but you may be so far down the marital cascades that you can't do it on your own. If you find you are extremely frustrated in trying the strategies for marital change described in this book, you may need professional help from a marital therapist. There is nothing at all wrong with getting this help. After all, your problems were not created overnight, and it is unreasonable to think that you can instantly turn around problems that have a long history. If you feel completely stuck, getting help is smart. I encourage you to seek professional help with problems that are too hard to solve on your own, and to use this book in tandem with marital therapy.

Sadly, it could also be the case that your marriage is simply beyond repair. One sign of this may be if you or your spouse cling to feelings of bitterness, hurt, and anger that are inconsolable. You or your spouse may be holding on to bitterness, as if to say, "What you did to me is so bad I won't ever forgive it and go on. I won't let myself be consoled." If there is such bitterness in your marriage, it makes it extremely difficult to change things. Changing your marriage requires commitment to do so from both you and your spouse. Without that the task may be impossible.

Knowing when a marriage is over is also important. Not all couples should stay together, and sometimes separation or divorce is a better alternative to continued conflict, depression, loneliness, and despair.

If you do decide to divorce, remember that most people who do so eventually remarry. My hope is that, if you do begin again, you will use the insights in this book to build a strong and healthy emotional partnership from the start.

A FINAL WORD

I hope by now you have a clear sense of how marriages can continue to thrive throughout the years, and what you can do if yours seems to be ailing. Anyone who has experienced an unhappy marriage knows how painful and demoralizing it can be. But please remember that many marriages are salvageable even when they seem most hopeless.

If your marriage is in trouble, there are any number of other marriage manuals or counselors you can turn to for help. Some of their advice will be sound, some of little value. What makes the information in this book unique is that it is based on actual, intensive scientific study of hundreds of couples. My goal has been to share with you what I have learned from my research about why some marriages fail while others thrive, and to show you how to use the wisdom we have gathered to save or improve your own union.

When things get complicated between you and your spouse—when every conversation becomes subsumed by nasty arguments, broken records, wheels within wheels, or cold silence—the solution isn't necessarily complicated. Many people in troubled marriages will say, "We just can't communicate" or "We're not on the same wavelength." But almost all adults (including your spouse!) are able to communicate effectively and resolve conflicts, as evidenced by their ability to make friends, work well with others, and have satisfactory relations with their neighbors. So why does communication in marriage become so difficult? The answer is that the more overwhelmed by negativity your relationship becomes, the less access either of you has to your natural talents for resolving differences.

A certain degree of negativity is crucial to a marriage. Without it, a marriage will surely deteriorate over time. But when the negativity level gets too high, the marriage inevitably suffers. I hope this book has helped you see how excess negativity can slowly infiltrate even a very happy marriage, creating blocks between a loving husband and wife before they realize what is happening. Remember that there are proven antidotes if your relationship is becoming overwhelmed by negativity. The first is to keep the four horsemen at bay by avoiding being critical, contemptuous, defensive, or stonewalling during disagreements. Be aware of negative inner thoughts, which can become entrenched into an ongoing mental script as the four horsemen settle in. Recognize when you or your spouse has become flooded, and give your body time to calm down before continuing a difficult discussion. Learn to listen and to speak nondefensively. Make sure your day-to-day lives include a good deal of validation and other expressions of love and respect. Most of all, work hard to *overlearn* all of the skills I have just mentioned. Validation and healthy approaches to resolving conflict need to become second nature so they won't abandon you when you need them most.

I do believe that by mastering these skills you can stop or prevent your relationship from tumbling down the cascade toward marital breakdown. Instead, you will naturally settle into one of the three stable marital styles my research has uncovered: volatile, validating, or avoidant. You will be able to look back at your marital history with pride—glorifying in the struggles you went through as a couple (including the rocky times that may have led you to this book!) and will look toward the future with happy anticipation.

Wherever your marital journey takes you, I wish you years of joy and pleasure together—spiced with just enough negativity to keep your marriage strong.

ACKNOWLEDGMENTS

I have been writing books and scientific articles about marriage for a long time now, but this is really the first attempt I have ever made at communicating the results to the general public, something I really didn't know how to do very well. I wouldn't have been able to do it without the help and guidance of Daniel Goleman. This book was written in collaboration with him and with several other writers with whom Dan and I worked, particularly Nan Silver, who edited the book into a seamless whole, and Joan DeClaire, Peggy Gillespie, and Carole Perkin. Holly Price Crowell in my laboratory ably guided the writing by making transcripts and data available to the writers.

Like this book, my research over the past twenty-one years has been a collaborative enterprise, beginning with my two excellent students, Howard Markman and Cliff Notarius, and continuing with my students Lowell Krokoff, Lynn Fainsilber Katz, Regina Rushe, and Joanne Wu Shortt. In the early years I followed a research methodology broadly outlined by my thesis advisor at the University of Wisconsin, Richard McFall. McFall suggested that clinical researchers be ethologists like Von Frisch who studied bees. These researchers should objectively observe the variability in natural behavior. The trick lay,

McFall suggested, in defining the situations to be studied and finding "competent populations" similar to the clinical population of interest. Much of this methodology remained to be worked out. That was easy in the area of marriage. In fact, much of the measurement work for defining couples who were satisfied or dissatisfied with their marriages had already been done.

The research enterprise has also involved important scholars at other laboratories, including Jim Sackett, Roger Bakeman, Robert Weiss, Gayla Margolin, Marion Forgatch, Geral Patterson, Hyman Hops, Carolyn and Philip Cowan, John Vincent, David Reiss, Joy Schulterbrand, Ross Parke, Gary Birchler, Dirk Revenstorf, Kurt Hahlweg, Caas Schaap, and more recently Laura Carstensen in our collaborative study of older, long-term marriages, and Neil Jacobson, in our collaboration in studying violent marriages. Harold Rausch and his work have a special place in providing ideas and inspiration to continue. I also wish to acknowledge the inspiration and support of Mavis Hetherington. Paul Ekman and Wallace Friesen were very important in guiding me along the way in my study of emotion.

Above all is my colleague and best friend, Bob Levenson, with whom I have had an intimate collaboration for the past fourteen years. Words cannot express the importance of this association to me.

I have been fortunate to have the assistance and insights of excellent coders, among them Mary Lynn Fletcher, Gwendolyn Mettetal, Mary Verdier, and most recently Kim McCoy, Carol Hooven, Christy Loberg, Sonny Ruckstahl, Jim Coan, Sherry Doggett, Coleen Conroy, Colleen Seto, and David McIntyre. Kim Buehlman made a major contribution to this research by designing the Oral History Coding System. Regina Rushe made a major contribution with her methodology when couples are interviewed about their most positively and most negatively rated moments.

Discussions with my wife, Julie Schwartz Gottman, who is a clinical psychologist, have been very influential; she is an insightful psychologist and a keen observer. This book is dedicated to her, not only for her insights into marital interaction but also because it is delightful to be married to her.

I want to thank the assistance and support of a very talented, loyal, and energetic secretary, Sharon Fentiman. She is a gifted artist and a very organized person and I am always amazed that she has decided to work with me and to put up with an organizationally impaired person.

I want to thank the infallible intuitions of my editor at Simon and Schuster, Gary Luke. He seems to be always right. I thank him for his guidance and constructive criticism.

This work would not have been possible without the continuing support of research grants from the National Institute of Mental Health, and Research Career Development awards and a Research Scientist Award I have held since 1979. The MacArthur Foundation paid for some of the construction costs of my apartment and fixed labs at the CDMRC.

Finally I sincerely want to thank the hundreds of couples who have participated in this research. They trusted us with the most intimate details of their lives, and theirs is really the major contribution toward this effort. They and not the researchers are the experts on marriage. It was our job to listen and to try to understand them. They did the living. They had the passions, the travails, the insights that have guided us. What they graciously donated to the research effort was the most private and sacred place in their lives. If any good comes of all this work, theirs will have to be recognized as the bravest and most important contribution of all.

JOHN MORDECHAI GOTTMAN
Seattle, Washington
1993